HAUNTED FORT SMITH & VAN BUREN

HAUNTED FORT SMITH & VAN BUREN

BUD STEED

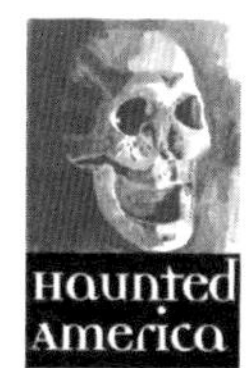

Published by Haunted America
A Division of The History Press
Charleston, SC
www.historypress.com

First published 2018

Manufactured in the United States

ISBN 9781467140706

Library of Congress Control Number: 2018942452

Notice: The information in this book is true and complete to the best of our knowledge. It is offered without guarantee on the part of the author or The History Press. The author and The History Press disclaim all liability in connection with the use of this book.

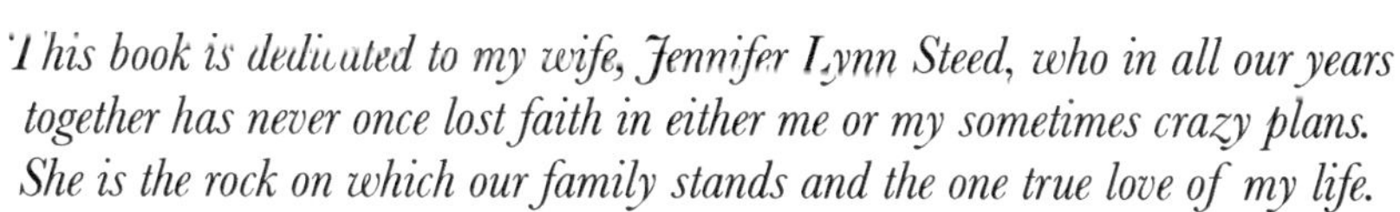

This book is dedicated to my wife, Jennifer Lynn Steed, who in all our years together has never once lost faith in either me or my sometimes crazy plans. She is the rock on which our family stands and the one true love of my life.

This book is also dedicated to my children:
Bobbi Jo, David, Sean, Ciara Jo and Kerra Lynn.
You all are great kids, and I cherish each of you more than you will ever know.

CONTENTS

Acknowledgments

I would like to acknowledge all the help and support that I obtained while writing this book.

First and foremost, I would like to thank my wife, Jennifer, for all the assistance that she gave to me while I was researching this book. From keeping me company during the long drives to waiting patiently while I conducted interviews or took photographs, your support, love, and companionship made the research behind this book extremely enjoyable. Also, special thanks to my son Sean Steed for riding shotgun with me on the numerous research trips to Fort Smith and Van Buren while I was taking additional photos for the book; the company was much appreciated.

I would also like to extend my thanks to Matt Wallace, Matthew Massey and everyone at SMC Packaging Group for their support. The willingness of everyone to stand there patiently while I rambled on about one haunting or another that I had just discovered, a paranormal investigation that I was about to embark on or my next book project is truly amazing—not to mention much appreciated.

Special thanks to my friends Adrian and Tina Scalf of River Valley Paranormal Research and Investigations (RVPRI) for taking the time to speak with me and share some of the history of the area and some interesting stories of the alleged hauntings for which the area is known; your knowledge and time are greatly appreciated.

Last but not least, thanks to everyone who shared their stories with me about their paranormal experiences in the Fort Smith and Van Buren areas. It was great fun speaking with all of you and hearing your stories.

Disclaimer

While I have strived to ensure the accuracy of the stories and the history behind them, I think that it is important to remember that they are indeed just ghost stories. Whether they are factual or not is impossible to say, as no one has ever proven the existence of life after death. When possible, I have included in the stories personal experiences obtained during investigations and research trips, but those are in no way definitive proof that a haunting is going on at a particular site. It simply means I had an experience that I couldn't debunk or find a logical answer for. Additionally, those stories that I can find very little truth behind, or are questionable at best in regard to any factual basis, are still included. Even if they are nothing more than an urban legend, they are still entertaining and show the process and evolution of the storytelling and legends associated with the area.

As those of you who have read my previous works already know, I make it a practice to change the names of the people in the book who shared their stories with me. While it is one thing for them to share their experiences with me one on one, I have never felt like that gives me the right to "out them" in a public venue such as this book. So, in order to share with you their stories as well as ensure that I do not cause them any embarrassment or ridicule, I simply change their names. It keeps everyone happy and eliminates any discomfort that anyone might have in relation to the story being told.

All in all, I hope that you enjoy this book and that the stories of ghosts and hauntings might move you to do a little investigating of your own to seek the truth behind the stories. It's a task that brings me great joy and fulfillment, as I am sure it will you as well. Read the stories, check into them a little further if you like and come to your own conclusions as to what is true and what is simply an urban legend, but above all else, just have fun with it and enjoy the stories!

Introduction

Both the Fort Smith and Van Buren areas have a rich and varied history, and with nothing but a river dividing the two, it's hard to talk about one without including the other. From early settlers to Civil War battles, from outlaws and lawmen to the everyday stresses and joys of daily living, they have all left their mark on the area in one form or another. Whether at historical sites or simply in the oral history associated with it, one thing comes prominently to the forefront: the paranormal.

Stories of ghosts and hauntings are commonplace in the Fort Smith and Van Buren areas, as they are in almost every area and culture in the world, and a lot of those center on violence and tragedy. The violence of the Civil War left its mark in the form of phantom soldiers that are sighted from time to time in the streets and buildings, as well as, in some cases, in the cemetery. The eighty-six death sentences carried out by hanging, seventy-nine of them the result of verdicts passed down by Judge Isaac Parker, are said to have produced phantoms still reliving their final moments on the gallows, seen briefly swaying in the mists and shadows near the old courthouse. Some are said to even inhabit the old courthouse itself, seen from time to time in the rooms and hallways—there one instant, gone the next, leaving witnesses wondering if they actually saw what they thought they did.

All in all, the rich history of the area produces some interesting stories and provides the ghost enthusiast with plenty of material to investigate. Let's start by taking a look at that history, first Fort Smith and then Van Buren, to get a better idea of why some of the stories of ghosts and hauntings exist.

A Brief History of Fort Smith

Situated on both the Arkansas River and what is now the border between Arkansas and modern-day Oklahoma, Fort Smith was once the last bastion of civilization before one set off into the wilds of the Indian Territory. First established as an outpost for westward exploration and then as a force to keep the peace between the Osages and the newly arrived Cherokees, who had been forcibly moved into the Indian Territory, Fort Smith occupied a high bluff, allowing soldiers to have an unrestricted view of the rivers and the lands around them.

The first Fort Smith was established on December 25, 1817, at Belle Point and was commanded by Major William Bradford. Because of its location by the rivers, as well as the extreme heat of summer and frigid winters, sickness was a very real threat that the occupants of the fort had to deal with. Deaths from fevers, pneumonia and dysentery were common, along with deaths from accidents and fighting. Life was hard for the troops stationed at Fort Smith in the early years.

The fort was briefly abandoned in the early 1820s, but the removal of the Five Civilized Tribes from the Southeast saw the army once again take up residence on Belle Point. Just briefly—as entire books could be and have been written on the subject—the Indian Removal Act called for the Five Civilized Tribes (Cherokee, Choctaw, Creek, Seminole and Chickasaw) to be rounded up and forcibly moved in sixteen detachments of about one thousand people each to the Indian Territory. They traveled mostly by overland routes, later referred to as "Nunahi-Duna-Dlo-Hilu-I," or "Trail Where They Cried"—we call it the Trail of Tears today. It's well known that thousands of people died along the trail due to illness and weather conditions such as drought and severe cold. Once they entered the Indian Territory, they were met by detachments from Fort Gibson and Fort

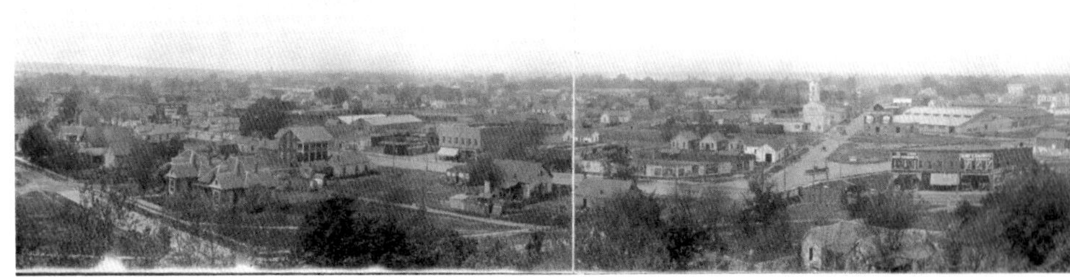

Smith. They were then directed to established tribal communities with other members of their nations who had arrived earlier, where they waited on the assignment of land parcels.

By 1838, a new Fort Smith was under construction, and the busy town of Fort Smith was growing by leaps and bounds along the eastern edge of Belle Point. The plans for the new fort called for twelve-foot-high stone walls that enclosed an area about four hundred by six hundred feet, with a two-story blockhouse at each corner. The task was a huge one, and it wouldn't be until 1846 that the fort was ready to be occupied. The army occupied the new fort up until the Civil War when Confederate forces took command of it in 1861. They held it until September 1863, when Union troops once again took control. Several battles would be fought around the immediate Fort Smith area, but the Confederates never again gained control of the fort. After the war, the military significance of the fort decreased with the westward expansion, and eventually, in the early 1870s, the United States Court for the Western District of Arkansas was moved from Van Buren to the old fort.

From 1873 until 1896, the federal court conducted eighty-six executions by hanging on the grounds of the old courthouse. One of the most famous people associated with Fort Smith was "Hanging Judge" Isaac Parker. Appointed in May 1875, he handed down 160 death sentences over his twenty-one-year term presiding over the court. Of those sentences, 43 were commuted to life sentences or reduced sentences. Two men saw presidential pardons, thirty-one saw their convictions overturned, two were granted new trials, one was shot and killed while trying to escape and two died in jail while they were waiting to be executed. The remaining seventy-nine men

Panoramic view of Fort Smith in 1910, from the Haines Photo Company Collection. *Courtesy of the Library of Congress.*

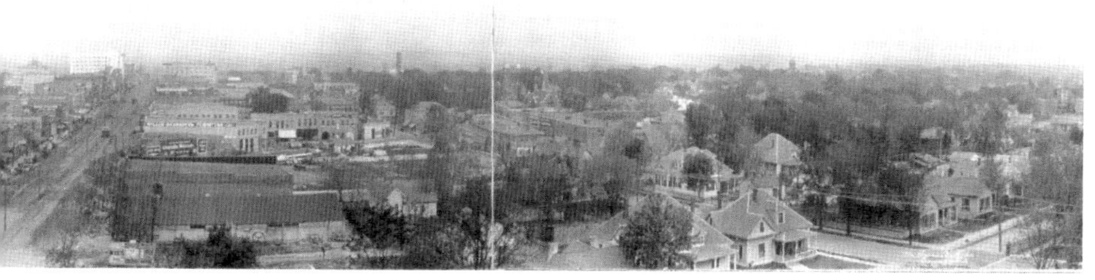

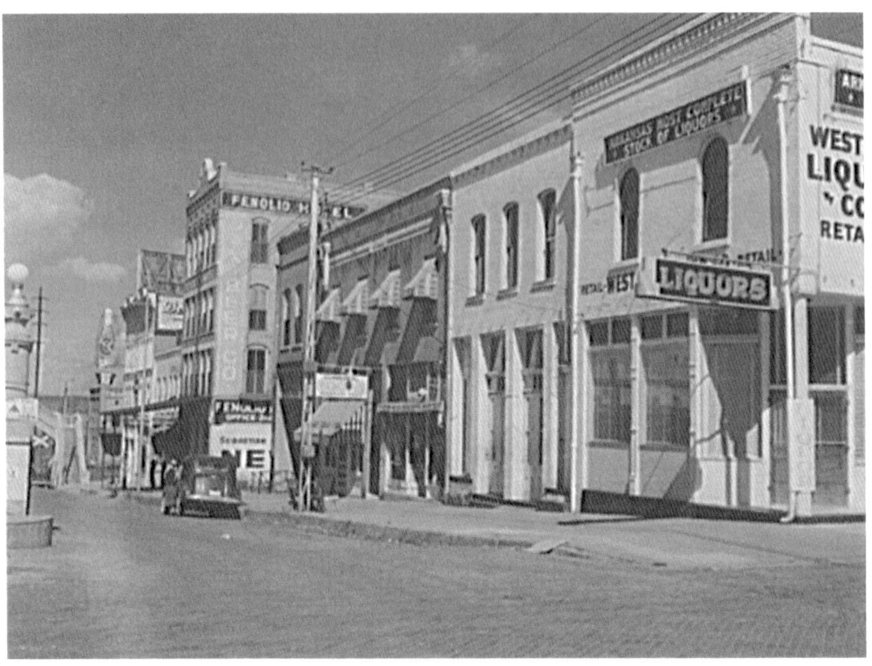

Street view of Fort Smith, 1942. *Courtesy of the Library of Congress.*

were hanged on the gallows at Fort Smith by the special deputy in charge of the executions, George Maledon. He served in that capacity for twenty-two years and became known as the "Prince of the Hangmen." On September 3, 1875, he would hang six men at once, earning Judge Parker's court the nickname "Court of the Damned." It's said that some of those who were executed are still "hanging around" the old courthouse area.

In 1896, the federal court lost its jurisdiction over the Indian Territory, leaving the gallows useless. Almost one year later, they were dismantled and burned. By 1957, the courthouse had been improved and Judge Parker's courtroom reconstructed, and today a reconstruction of the gallows, completed in the early 1980s, stands on the original spot.

The town of Fort Smith grew rapidly alongside the fort itself, and by the late 1880s, it had almost tripled in population. Manufacturing facilities were established in the glass and furniture industries, and from the 1950s to the 1970s, the manufacturing base grew to include such notable employers as Whirlpool and Baldor Electric Company.

In 1942, Camp Chaffee was activated just east of Fort Smith, and the army built three POW compounds totaling about fifty-three acres to house

German prisoners. It would later be renamed Fort Chaffee, and in the 1980s, it would become the site of a Cuban refugee camp, housing more than nineteen thousand people. Riots, prostitution, and violence were rampant during those days in the refugee camp.

Today, Fort Smith is the second-largest city in Arkansas, boasting a population in excess of eighty-six thousand people. Beautiful parks, historic sites and districts and excellent educational facilities combine to make this once frontier town a first-class place to call home.

A Brief History of Van Buren

Situated on the opposite side of the Arkansas River from Fort Smith, Van Buren started life around 1818 as a small settlement clustered around a boat landing. The year 1819 saw the arrival of Daniel and Thomas Phillips, who would eventually establish a woodlot from which they supplied the flatboats traveling the river with fuel for their steam engines. The town would come to be known as Phillips Landing, and by 1831, it boasted a post office named after Secretary of State Martin Van Buren, the woodlot, and a small trading post. At the same time, a short distance downstream from the landing, the town of Columbus had sprung up, centered on a ferry operation and a few small stores. In 1836, two of the founders of Columbus, John Drennan and David Thompson, decided that Phillips Landing was a better townsite since it sat much higher. They bought the townsite from Thomas Phillips for $11,000 and proceeded to survey and layout the town properly.

In 1838, it officially became the seat of Crawford County, the city square being donated around 1841 by both Drennan and Thompson, with the building of the Crawford County Courthouse to come a short time later. By 1845, the city of Van Buren had become officially incorporated. The town grew rapidly, and by 1849, the population had doubled, in part due to the influx of travelers bound for the California gold fields. It now had several stores, a wharf and riverfront warehouse, a flour mill and a bathhouse.

The year 1851 saw the creation of the First District Court of Arkansas at Van Buren, where it would operate until the early 1870s, at which point it was moved to Fort Smith. With the outbreak of the Civil War, Van Buren and the area around it saw numerous battles and skirmishes, and by the end of December 1862, Van Buren had come under Union control.

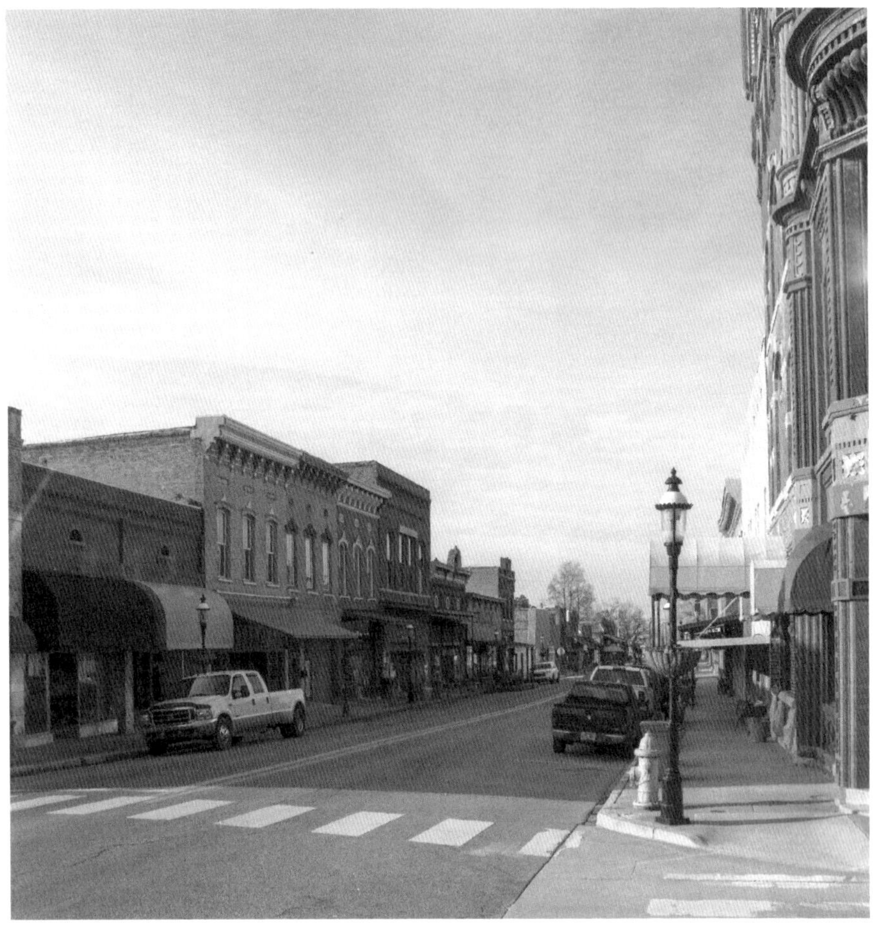

Van Buren's historic Main Street district. *Photo by Bud Steed.*

The 1880s and the years after saw the opening of a passenger train connecting Van Buren to the Rogers/Fayetteville areas; the opening of two opera houses, one of which, the King Opera House, is still standing today; and eventually a bridge connecting Van Buren with Fort Smith, eliminating the need for the ferry service that had been the only connecting route between the two cities. Fast-forward to the World War II era and we find the activation of Camp Johnson, later renamed Camp Jesse Turner, a fifty-three-acre military railroad facility along with a USO facility to service the military from both bases. After the war years, Van Buren continued to experience good growth with the state's first port authority and the establishment of manufacturing, transportation and food preparation facilities such as Tyson Foods, Allen Canning, and Simmons Foods.

Van Buren continues to be a popular destination for tourists, and with its 135-acre park system, the Center for Art and Education and an exceptional school system, it's also a great place to raise a family.

As you can see, both cities have interesting histories. As with most places established during this period, this location was a wild and sometimes dangerous area filled with outlaws, military battles, and skirmishes, as well as no small amount of death, bloodshed, and despair. Add to those the loss, joys, happiness and daily living and dying that goes along with trying to eke out a living in a frontier town and it's no small wonder that both places have more than their fair share of hauntings and ghost stories. I've decided to break down the rest of the book into two broad parts. The first part will cover the hauntings and ghost stories associated with Fort Smith and the second part will cover Van Buren. I had originally intended to add a third part to the book that would contain stories centered on the outlying areas—those within a twenty- to thirty-mile radius of the Fort Smith and Van Buren areas. Ultimately, though, I decided to tell those stories (and a few more that didn't really fit into the geographical area of the book but that had a connection to the area) through my blog located on my website (budsteed.com) as supplemental material to this book—sort of as a bonus for you, the reader. While the outlying areas might not have the long history behind them that the two larger areas have, even small towns have some interesting stories to tell.

PART I

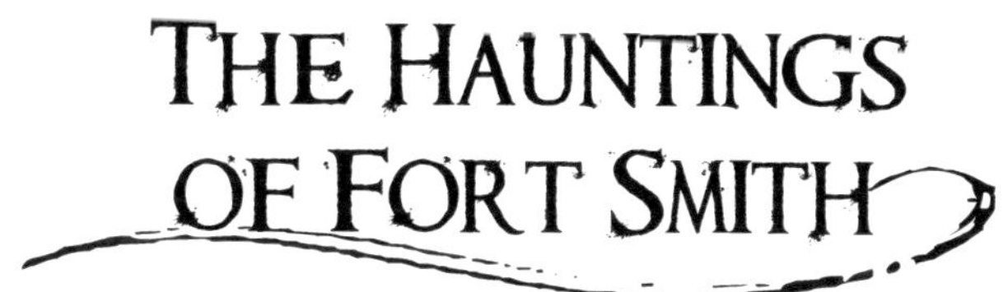

The Hauntings of Fort Smith

Fort Smith has a lot to offer to those who are interested in the paranormal. With its military history, prison, refugee camps, the hangings by "Hanging Judge" Isaac Parker and a well-restored historic district that seems to have a few former residents that just can't move on, the city is chock-full of interesting stories and places just waiting to be investigated. When possible, I've tried to include some of my own findings regarding the alleged paranormal activity, as well as to stay faithful to the stories told to me by those who believe they had a paranormal experience. I've also tried to include insights, evidence and accounts from local area paranormal researchers and investigators like Adrian and Tina Scalf of River Valley Paranormal Research and Investigations. They have had the good fortune of investigating a number of locations within the Fort Smith and Van Buren areas and bring a unique perspective to the stories of the ghosts and hauntings.

So, is Fort Smith haunted? Maybe. I'm afraid you will have to read the accounts that follow and come to your own conclusions about that.

THE CLAYTON HOUSE

Built in 1852 by a man named Sutton, what is now known as the Clayton House started life on a slightly smaller scale. It wasn't until the home was purchased in 1876 by William Henry Harrison Clayton, then the federal prosecuting attorney for Judge Isaac Parker, that the home took on the appearance that you see today. Clayton moved his family into the home in 1882 after renovating it in the Victorian Gothic/Italianate style and doubling the size of the house. Coming in at slightly more than six thousand square feet of living space, the house boasted a study, a sitting room, a formal parlor, a dining room and four upstairs bedrooms with a common living area dividing them. William and his wife, Florence, would reside in the home until 1897 when William would be appointed judge of the United States Court of the Central District of the Indian Territory in McAlester, located in what would later become the state of Oklahoma.

While in Fort Smith, William and Florence raised six daughters and one son and enjoyed a respected and popular private and public life. William was active in both Freemasonry and the Knights Templar organizations, serving in leadership positions in both, while Florence helped found the Fortnightly Club. The Fortnightly Club was a ladies' literary and social club and is credited with helping to establish the first public library in Fort Smith.

When the Claytons moved to McAlester, they took much of their furnishings along with them; however, the home does boast a few of their original furniture items, such as Florence's writing desk and a tea table. Also on display are William's walking stick, numerous photos, and the family

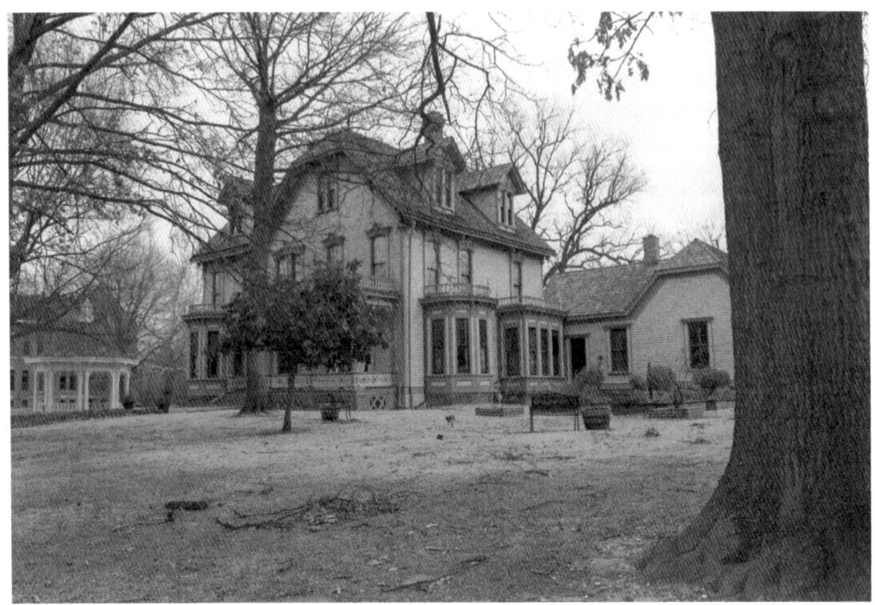

Side view of the Clayton House in Fort Smith. William H.H. Clayton was the prosecuting attorney for Judge Isaac Parker. *Photo by Bud Steed.*

Bible. The rest of the furnishings, with the exception of the piano and pump organ, were donated from the estate of a Mrs. Agnes Oglesby, who I learned from taking the tour of the house actually knew the Claytons and had been to their home numerous times. I was told that Mrs. Oglesby, who passed away in 1979, was a treasure-trove of information during the restoration of the home, giving firsthand accounts of colors and decorations within the home and helping to ensure the authenticity of the restoration.

Over the years, the home served many purposes. After Sutton, the original owner and builder departed for Texas at the start of the Civil War, the house was used as a Union hospital, then later as the home of the Claytons and eventually saw service as a boardinghouse for a bit when it was owned by a lady named Emma High. It's thought that several of the spirits alleged to haunt the home could be from the Civil War hospital days or from when it was a boardinghouse. To my knowledge, though, no one has ever confirmed either thought. Many people over the years have reported seeing apparitions, experiencing odd smells, being touched and even having their hair pulled. After the tour of the home, my wife and I asked the tour guide, a charming and very knowledgeable young lady named Amy, if she had ever experienced anything paranormal while working at the house. She was a bit

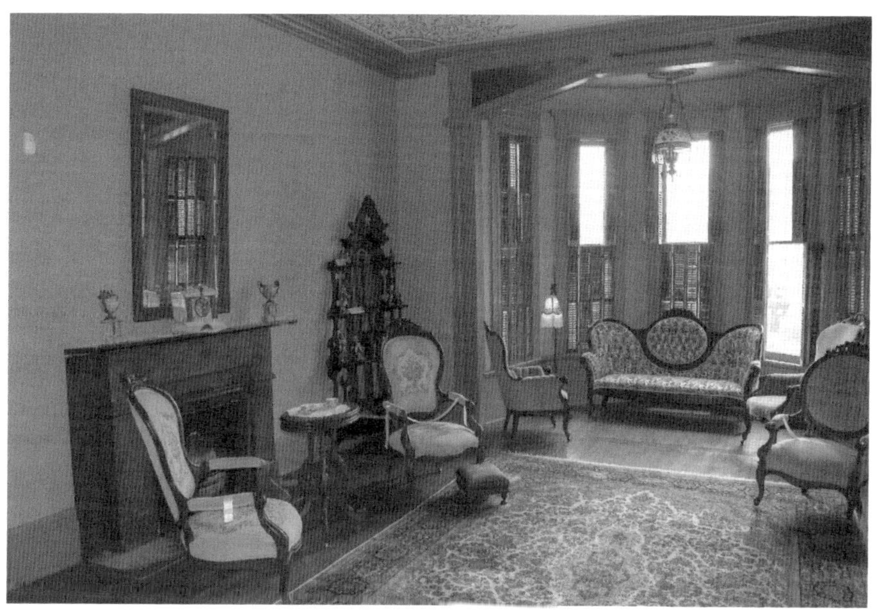

Front parlor of the Clayton House. Guests would have been received here. *Photo by Bud Steed.*

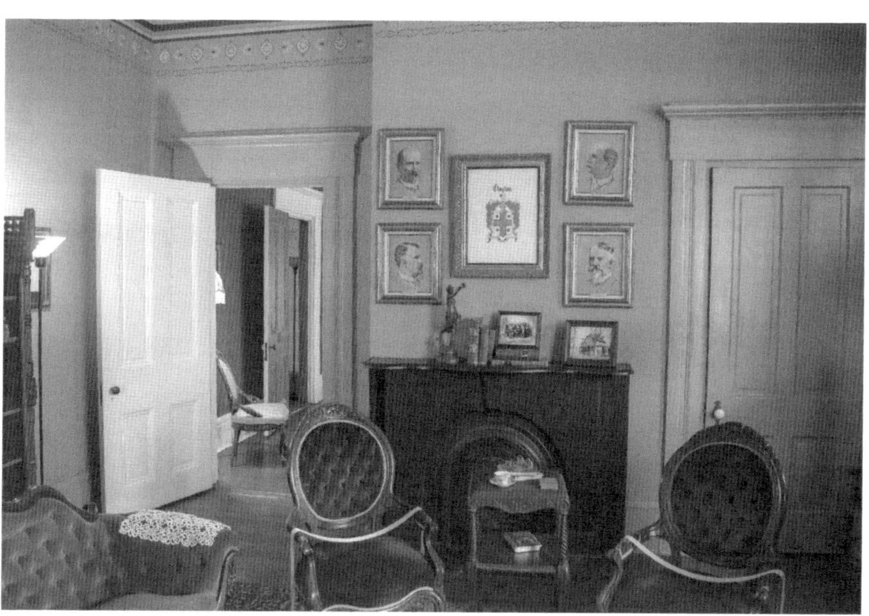

William H.H. Clayton's study. After dinner, the men would have gathered here to smoke and have a drink or two. *Photo by Bud Steed.*

hesitant at first, but after a moment, she related an encounter with an unseen pipe-smoking entity.

Amy had been working in the office, which is located at the back of the home when she thought she smelled something burning—an odd type of smell that was unfamiliar to her. She searched all throughout the house, checking to make sure that nothing was on fire. Finding nothing that would account for the smell, she went back to the office to continue her work, but while passing through the study, she once again smelled the odd smoky odor. While standing there trying to figure out where it was coming from, she realized that it seemed to be all around her but concentrated just in the study, not in the adjoining rooms. At about that time, a maintenance worker who was doing some restoration work outside came in for a moment, and she asked him if he smelled the smoke as well. He said that he did and that it smelled like high-end pipe tobacco. A bit nervous now, she half-jokingly asked whoever it was that was smoking if they would refrain from doing it in the house and while she was working. Within moments, the smell of pipe tobacco completely disappeared, and she has never experienced it since. I found it interesting that the smell was confined only to the study, an area that would have seen perhaps Mr. Clayton or one of his guests relaxing in conversation while smoking a pipe and enjoying a brandy after dinner—a place of relaxation away from the business of law and prosecution. Perhaps he enjoyed his refuge so much that he comes back from time to time to continue enjoying it, or perhaps it's someone else entirely. One thing is for certain: whoever it might have been, he was a gentleman who obviously honored the wishes of a lady.

The Angry Man

One of the spirits alleged to haunt the Clayton House is that of the "Angry Man." Said to be a tall man dressed in black, no one has been able to identify him or his attachment to the house. Speculation is that he was either a doctor or soldier who was at the house at the time that it was a Union hospital during the Civil War, but no one really knows for sure, as interaction with him has been brief at best.

He seems to frequent the upstairs landing area and bedrooms adjacent to the stairs most of the time, but he has been seen on the porch and in various other places throughout the home from time to time. The stomping footsteps, like someone walking in heavy boots, have been attributed to the Angry Man in black, as he seems to pace the floor with impatience.

While touring the home, I caught a glimpse of what I believe was the man on several occasions, catching the movement of someone tall and dressed in black walking on the stairs and the upstairs landing out of the corner of my eye. I also felt as though I was being watched the entire time I was in the house, but not in a hostile, "you're intruding so I'm keeping my eye on you" sort of way, but more along the lines of curiosity, as if someone was wondering why I was there and what I was going to do next. I should include here that not once did I feel any type of threatening vibe at all. My impression, for what it's worth, and I'm no psychic medium by any means, was that the so-called Angry Man wasn't necessarily angry at anyone in particular but more or less peeved at the situation that he was in, if that makes any sense. I've learned to trust the instincts that I've developed over thirty-eight years of paranormal investigation, and I can honestly say that I didn't feel anything threatening or malevolent in any way while I was in the house.

One story associated with the man in black was told to me by a young woman who was a guest at a wedding held at the home. Janet was attending the wedding of a friend and had chosen to stand at the back during the ceremony. While the couple was exchanging their vows, she happened to notice a man dressed in a black suit, the old-fashioned kind that had the long coat, standing a few feet to her left, his hands clasped behind his back. She thought he looked a little odd with the old-time suit and the bushy beard, but she put the thought out of her mind, concentrating on the wedding vows being exchanged. When she glanced back a moment later, the man was nowhere to be seen. She looked behind her and to her right, but the man was simply gone. Shrugging it off, she went back to watching the wedding, trying not to cry a little, as she said she almost always cries at weddings. A few seconds later, as she was dabbing at her eyes with a tissue, she heard someone directly behind her clear his throat. She said it startled her, and she sort of spun around, caught a little off guard, as just a few moments earlier there hadn't been anyone even close to her. Standing just a few feet away from her was the man dressed in the black suit again, watching the wedding rather intently. Janet sort of smiled and looked directly at the man and said something to the effect of, "You startled me," but she said he just stood there, silently watching the ceremony. Thinking that he was more than just a little rude, she thought about saying something when he turned his head and looked at her. She said he had a rather sad look on his face and that as their eyes locked, he slightly nodded his head, smiled at her and then vanished right before her eyes.

To say that Janet was taken aback would be an understatement. She said she just stood there for a moment with her mouth open in disbelief, not believing what she had just seen but knowing full well that she had. She stayed for the rest of the wedding and the reception but never saw the man in black again. She told me that he had the saddest eyes of anyone she had ever seen, sort of like his heart was breaking while he was watching the wedding—like he was filled with some type of remorse or something. She couldn't quite put her finger on the feeling she got from him, but he was definitely extremely sad about something.

Janet has been back to the Clayton House several times since then, always hoping to catch a glimpse of the man that vanished before her eyes, but so far she has never encountered him again.

The Lady in Brown

Another story associated with the Clayton House is that of the Lady in Brown. She has been seen several times, usually in the study or in the sitting room, and usually, she is simply standing there looking out the window. Dressed in a long brown skirt and white linen high-necked blouse buttoned all the way up, with her gray hair put up neatly in a bun on the top of her head, she is reported to be the very figure of a proper Victorian lady. As with most spirits, it seems that no one is quite sure who she is, as she doesn't seem to interact with anyone, but one theory is that she might be Emma High, who once owned the home while it was a boardinghouse; another theory is that she might be none other than Florence Clayton herself.

Most people who have seen her state that she doesn't seem to be aware of anyone, which leads me to believe that she is simply a residual haunting—a "place memory" or energy that, for some unknown reason, appears from time to time in pretty much the same place doing the same thing. Rather like a video recording set to replay again and again in a continuous loop, the event exhibits no intelligence, no interaction and no awareness, just a brief appearance and then disappearance.

Those who have seen her state that she seems very poised and almost serene, standing quietly, looking out the window. Then she is simply gone without a trace as if someone had flipped a switch and turned her off like a lamp. No fading from sight, no turning around and then vanishing—just gone in the blink of an eye. One thing that is confusing for me is that she seems to be so calm. Most residual hauntings are associated with some traumatic event that happened that left an impression on the place, to be played over again and again, but by all accounts, she seems to be peacefully looking out the window. Perhaps she's not a residual haunting at all but just doesn't feel the need to acknowledge anyone else's presence or simply wishes to be left alone.

Other Experiences

While the Angry Man in black and the lady in the brown dress seem to be the spirits encountered the most at the Clayton House, there have been other unexplained happenings that have left people bewildered. More than one person has reported the sounds of music and soft singing while in the house when no radio of any type was present at the time.

One of the tour guides related that she was in the office doing a bit of work when she heard the front door open and close. Thinking that someone had walked in looking to take the tour, she called out that she would be right with them. As she got up from the desk, she could clearly hear the sounds of someone walking quickly up the stairs, which caused her to call out again, asking the person to please wait downstairs, that the tours were guided only. No one answered, and the footsteps seemed to stop at the top of the stairs.

Thinking that perhaps the person simply hadn't heard her call out, she hurried up the stairs to catch them. At the top of the stairs, there was no one visible, and a quick check of the rooms revealed that there was no one up there but her. Perplexed, she paused at the top of the stairs for a moment and clearly heard what sounded like a man humming a tune. Knowing that there was no one upstairs, she beat a hasty retreat back down to the office and stayed there for the rest of her shift, noting from time to time the sounds of someone pacing back and forth upstairs.

On a separate occasion, the same tour guide had just finished a tour and saw the last person out the door. Turning from the door, she went over and sat down for a moment on the bottom stair step just to take a break. While sitting there, she started to notice what sounded like a woman's voice, very low and almost at a whisper. As she strained to hear the voice more clearly, it started to get louder and was easily recognizable as someone softly singing a song, almost the way someone would do as they went about some chore. As she listened, she could make out some of the words: "Please let mother come home again. We want her, daddy and I. Please let mother come home again. Back from your beautiful sky." She promptly went into the office and wrote them down. A quick Google check of the words brought her to a website called Parlor Songs and showed them to be from a song called "Please Let Mother Come Home Again," written in 1892. I looked up the Parlor Songs website and verified that the words she heard being softly sung that afternoon were indeed from this song, written by Robert Donnelly. Apparently, it was quite a popular song back then.

A former volunteer related a story to me about piano music. She was upstairs doing some light cleaning when she heard what sounded like someone playing the piano downstairs. Thinking that someone had come in and she just hadn't heard them, she rushed downstairs to put a stop to whoever was messing with the piano. The piano, located in the sitting room, is a Mathushek orchestral square piano manufactured in 1884 and would be valued at between $35,000 and $40,000 (estimate only), so the thought of someone messing around with it was quite distressing to her. As she got to the bottom of the stairs, the music stopped, and when she rounded the corner, she drew up short, surprised to find no one there. A fast search of the downstairs showed that there was no one in the home but her at the time. A bit bewildered, she slowly went back upstairs to finish her chores. As she reached the top stairs, she once again heard the sound of the piano being played; she said she literally flew down the stairs to try and catch whoever it was, but once again, there was no one near the piano or even in the entire downstairs. More than a little shook up, she paused in the doorway to the sitting room and said aloud, "Please stop playing the piano. It's very expensive, and if anything was to happen to it, I would lose my ability to work here." With that, she turned around and went back upstairs to resume her work. She said she never heard the piano played again the entire time she worked there.

Another entity said to haunt the Clayton House is that of the ghost cat. From what I can gather, it is never really seen very much, although it has been glimpsed from time to time—it's more felt than anything else. Many people have felt the sensation of a cat rubbing up against their legs or running between their legs, whereupon they instinctively step wide to keep from stepping on it, even though they don't see it; some have even felt it jump against them. Both Tina and Adrian Scalf of RVPRI,

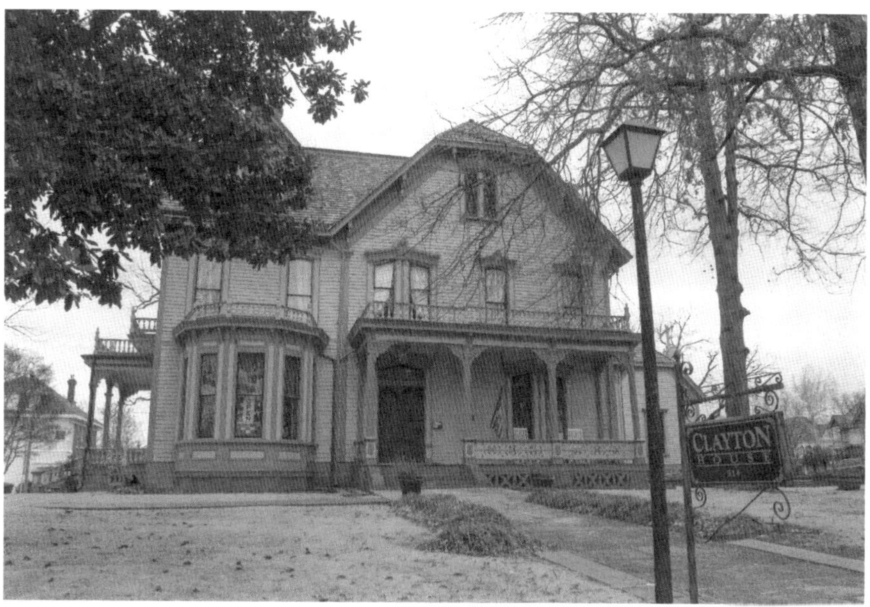

Front view of the Clayton House. *Photo by Bud Steed.*

who have investigated the Clayton House on several occasions, have experienced the ghost cat rubbing up against their legs, and they even caught an EVP of a cat meowing, even though there are no cats inside the house. The stories of ghost animals are quite common. The Crescent Hotel in Eureka Springs, Arkansas, has a ghost cat they call Morris that roams the property, so the possibility that the Clayton House has a ghost cat isn't that far-fetched.

There are a lot of stories associated with the Clayton House and a lot of history to provide the backstory for them. Quite a few people have reported experiences that they simply couldn't explain no matter how hard they tried, and the general consensus is that the place is indeed haunted. I tend to agree with the popular opinion. There are simply too many stories and accounts of paranormal activity to dismiss the possibility that it isn't haunted. I was informed at the end of our tour that they were going to be offering overnight private paranormal investigations; the price had not been decided, but it would undoubtedly help to cover the cost of someone from the home staying as a guide during the investigation. An investigation of the home is definitely on my bucket list for the near future, and any evidence and an account of the investigation will be posted on my website (budsteed.com) and on my team website (backroadsparanormal.com) for those who might be interested. I'll also be posting it on our other team website (infinityparanormalresearch.com) too, so there will be plenty of places for you to check out evidence and investigations as they pertain to the Clayton House and other locations mentioned in the book.

Old Fort Smith Courthouse and the Old Fort

Built on Belle Point at the confluence of the Arkansas and Poteau Rivers in 1817, the first Fort Smith was a structure of both logs and stone. It came into existence due to conflicts between the Osage and Cherokee tribes, who were feuding over land and hunting rights. It was abandoned in 1824, but a fear of Indian attacks, plus the ever-present problem of unscrupulous individuals making and selling whiskey in the Indian Territory, saw the fort being rebuilt in 1838. Today, only the stone foundations remain, along with a few historical markers and, curiously enough, a huge weathered and rusted iron "eye" ring sunk into the rock at the river's edge—perhaps the only reminder that boats used to tie up along the shore below the fort.

While there have been several reports of paranormal activity centered on the old fort area, the majority of reports seem to come from the area of the old commissary building, built between 1838 and 1846, and the old enlisted men's barracks, which would later become the courthouse. In 1849, the barracks would suffer from a destructive fire requiring a massive rebuild of the structure, and it continued to see use as housing for single enlisted men right up until the fort closed in 1871.

From 1872 until 1896, the former enlisted men's barracks was added onto and put to use as the courthouse, jail and U.S. Marshal's Office for the Federal Court of the Western District of Arkansas. The basement, which was once the mess hall for the troops stationed there, was converted into a jail with two large cells. The jail held up to fifty men per cell, had little to no ventilation and had a bucket that was used as the toilet; it earned the

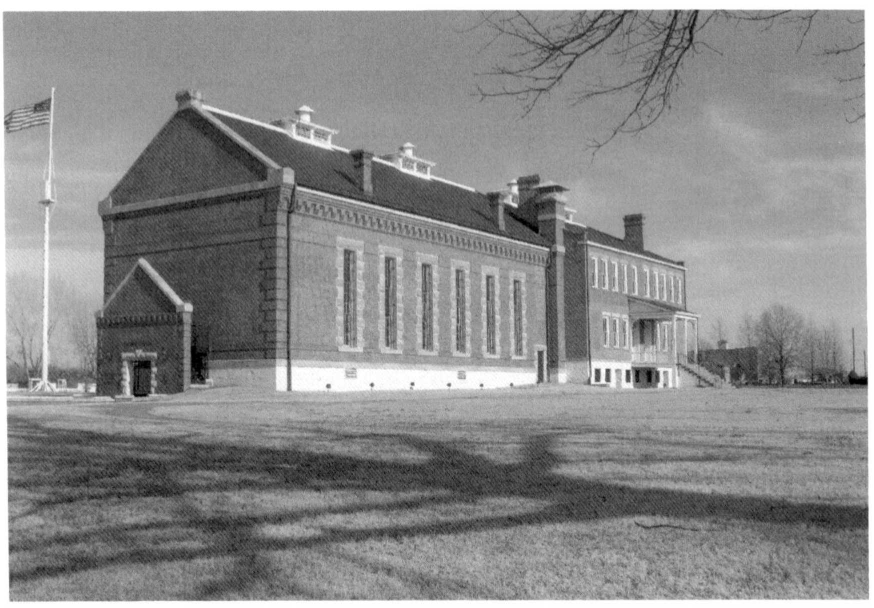

The historic Fort Smith Courthouse. It was originally soldiers' quarters when it was an active army fort and was later remodeled to hold the jail and Judge Parker's courtroom. *Photo by Bud Steed.*

nickname of "Hell on the Border" and rightly so. It was said that prisoners would conduct mock trials as something to do to relieve the boredom of their incarceration.

During its tenure as a court, it was the domain of "Hanging Judge" Isaac Parker, the federal judge tasked with the job of hearing cases and deciding the punishment that went with the verdict. He heard more than thirteen thousand cases, of which he sentenced 160 people to death by hanging, although due to appeals and retrials, only 79 were ever sent to the gallows. The gallows were located a short distance from the building, and a replica stands in the spot of the original today. The courtroom has also been restored to how it looked in Judge Parker's day, and the lower floor that once held the jail is now a visitors' center.

The commissary building was slated for demolition in 1909; however, it was saved and became the city's first history museum, serving in that capacity from 1910 to 1979. In Judge Parker's day, the second floor of the building was used in part as his office, with the first floor housing the court officers. Today, the bottom floor is set up as a commissary, with displays of goods stacked along the walls depicting how things might have looked

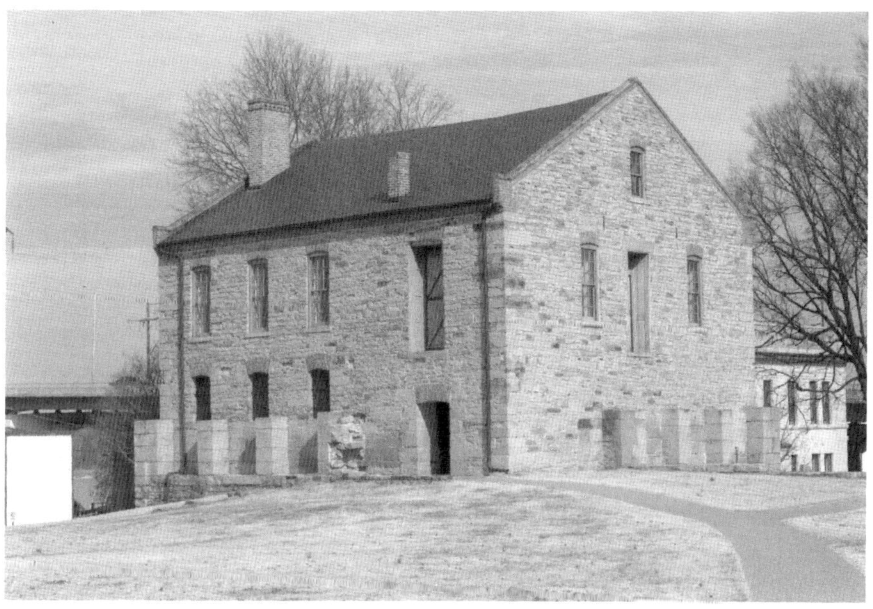

The restored commissary building. At one time, Judge Parker had offices on the second floor, and during a good portion of the 1900s, it was the area history museum. *Photo by Bud Steed.*

during the army days. The bottom floor is open to the public, but the upper floors are closed off. While we were there with Adrian and Tina Scalf of River Valley Paranormal Research and Investigations touring the grounds, the courthouse, and the commissary, I walked around the building taking photos and paused for a few moments just to take a really good look at the building. When I looked up at the upper-floor window, the one closest to the river, I distinctly saw a man in the window looking down at me. I snapped a few photos and didn't really think anything of it until I walked around the entire building and found that the doors to the upper level were padlocked; there were no other entrances inside or out where someone could have gained access, and the doors were padlocked from the outside. None of the photos I took showed anyone in the window, but I know what I saw. It's just one of those personal experiences that a lot of people seem to have around the old fort and the courthouse areas.

Hell on the Border Jail

Today, the bottom floor of the old courthouse building is home to the visitors' center, a display of old movie posters that mentioned or portrayed Fort Smith, the U.S. Marshal's Office/Judge Parker's office and a replica of what the original "Hell on the Border" jail looked like. Its original usage, back in the federal court days, was that of the jail. Conditions were less than stellar back then, with overcrowding, poor sanitary conditions and the smells of dozens of unwashed bodies packed into a small area with no ventilation to speak of—not a place you would want to hang out in. Most accounts state that only one man died in the actual jail itself while awaiting trial, while most of the other deaths happened on the gallows a short walk from the jail. With that being the case, one would have to wonder why anyone would want to hang out around there after they had died, but it does seem to be the case, as numerous accounts of paranormal activity have been reported. However, if you ask any of the park rangers working the visitors' center if they have ever experienced anything strange while in the building, most will simply pause for a moment, give you a long look and say no. That's the official statement. I did have several of the employees tell me off the record that they are supposed to deny any paranormal happenings, but that doesn't necessarily mean there aren't any. They were kind enough to share their experiences with me as long as I promised to keep their names out of it; no one wants to lose their jobs, and I certainly don't want to be the one responsible for getting anyone in trouble, hence the following false names.

Mary has been working at the park for somewhere around six to eight years now, and Linda has been working there for just a bit longer. Adam has only been working there for a few years, but he was pretty adamant about not liking to be in the building alone when it got dark. The ladies agreed with him 100 percent.

Mary related a story to me about sitting at the desk in the visitors' center and watching a man in western-style garb stroll right past her (tipping his hat as he went), pass through the closed doors and then disappear. She said he was young, had a bushy handlebar mustache and had a very amused look on his face as he looked at her. She said she just froze in place at the desk, not sure what to do, what to say or who to say it to. She finally decided to just simply do nothing; after all, who was going to believe her anyway?

Another story involved both Mary and Linda and took place in the jail area. They were both sitting at the reception desk when all of a sudden they heard what sounded like someone just dying of laughter—big, loud belly laughs, as Mary put it. Knowing that no one was in the building but them at the moment, they both got up and walked down the hall to the "Hell on the Border" jail area. As soon as they got to the doorway of the jail, the laughing stopped rather abruptly. Looking inside (the interior is one big room with nowhere anyone could hide), they saw that the room was empty. They sort of looked at each other and backed out of the room, stopping a few feet inside the hallway away from the door and standing up against the wall. After a moment or so, they started to hear clearly audible voices coming from inside the jail. It sounded as if two men were carrying on a conversation, and the conversation was about them! They both remembered it going something like this.

First man: "You think they are gone yet?"

Second man: "I don't think so. I think they are standing outside the door."

First man: "Well go look and see."

Second man: "You want to know, then walk your ass out there and look for yourself. I ain't going."

There was silence for a few moments. Mary and Linda just stood there, open-mouthed, looking at each other.

First man: "Well, I think you should go. It was you they heard laughing."

Second man: "Fine. I'll go and see, you scaredy cat!"

Both Mary and Linda swear that they could feel the temperature drop in the hallway as they were standing there against the wall, both afraid to move. After a few moments, the temperature started to warm back up, and they could hear the voices again, coming from the jail.

First man: "They still out there?"

Second man: "Yep. Still standing out there. They look a bit put out about something though. Kinda sour looks on their faces."

First man: "Well. What are we going to do about it?"

Second man: "I say we shoot 'em!"

With that, both Mary and Linda darted down the hallway toward the relative safety of the reception desk, the sounds of laughter echoing down the hallway after them. Once they regained their composure, they had to laugh about the whole thing too. They knew that there was no one in the jail area, as they had just checked inside, and knew that there was no one else inside the building but them at the moment. That the two spirits were just having a laugh at their expense was obvious, and both of them agreed after they had had a chance to think it over that it was kind of funny. It would seem that there are a few good-natured spirits hanging out from

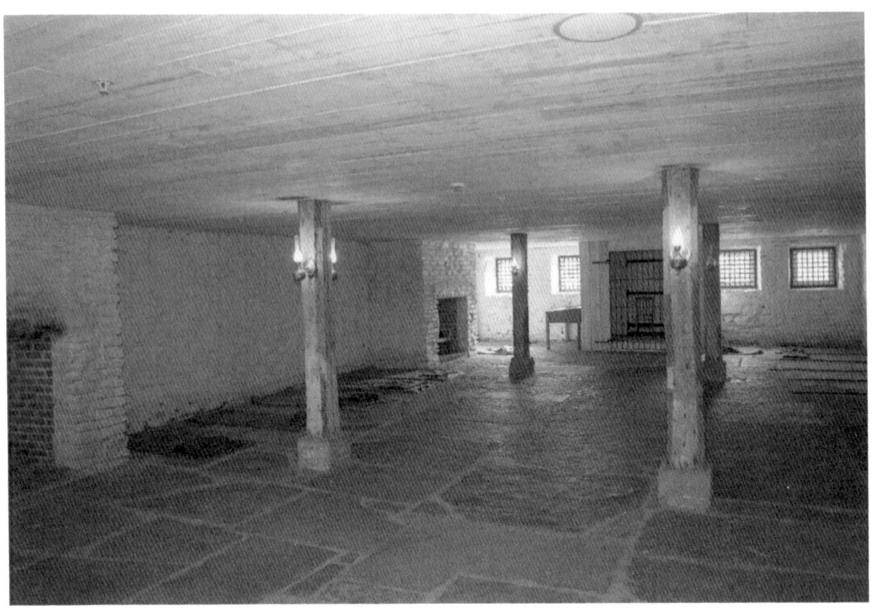

"Hell on the Border" jail. Up to fifty men would be held here at one time. *Photo by Bud Steed.*

time to time in the old jail area and that they appreciate a good laugh as much as the next person.

The ladies also reported that they will occasionally hear hushed voices coming from the jail area as if several people are engaged in some kind of conversation. It's always quiet, always when it's just the attendants at the reception desk and never goes on for long—just short snippets of an ongoing conversation.

Adam had an experience in the jail area as well. There are blankets arranged on the floor to mimic how they might have been arranged when the jail had actual prisoners residing there, and from time to time, careless visitors or their children will accidentally kick the blankets around, messing things up. Adam went in to check on things and saw the blankets messed up, so he went over and started straightening them out. About halfway through the third blanket, he noticed that it was suddenly much colder in the room. As he bent over to straighten the rest of the blanket, he felt a hard slap right on his behind, causing him to jump away and spin around to see who just slapped him on his butt. No one was there at all. He said he hurried up and finished straightening the blanket with his foot, looking all around him as he did, and when finished, he quickly departed the jail area, looking over his shoulder the whole way back to the reception desk. He said it certainly got his attention.

According to Linda, other people have reported being touched, having their hair pulled and their clothing tugged on; some have heard voices whispering in their ears. It's never anything malicious, just as if someone, or several someones, simply want to draw attention to the fact that they are still there. Mary thought that it was rather sad to think that after a person died they would have nowhere better to go than a basement jail in an old courthouse building. As she said, "If I was unfettered from this body and able to move around, I'd take off and see the world. I sure wouldn't spend eternity hanging out around here."

Judge Parker's Courtroom

Located at one end of the second floor of the old courthouse building, the courtroom of Judge Isaac Parker has been restored to its original glory. Filled with period lawyer's desks, hardback chairs in the jury box and an assortment of old books lining the shelves, the room looks much like it did when the "Hanging Judge" passed down his verdicts so many years ago. The room is really rather remarkable—you seem to step back in time from the moment you step foot into it. The lighting, the furnishings, the judge's bench set up high—it's all as if you walked in to take a seat as a spectator at one of the trials or, worst-case scenario, as a defendant.

Linda told me a story that was told to her by one of the cleaning staff who had been assigned to the courtroom. It was about 10:00 p.m., dark outside and was a cold and blustery winter night when the person had this experience. They had just entered the room, intent on starting their work by giving everything a good dusting when they noticed right off that there was a man sitting at one of the desks in front of the judge's bench. She excused herself, noting that she wasn't aware that there was anyone else left in the building other than the cleaning crew and the attendant downstairs, and turned to exit the room. That's when it dawned on her that the man was dressed in a dark, old-fashioned suit and had several books spread open before him. Thinking that maybe he was a period reenactor or someone left over from an event that day, she excused herself again and asked him who he was and what he was doing there since no one was allowed past the railing into the courtroom area.

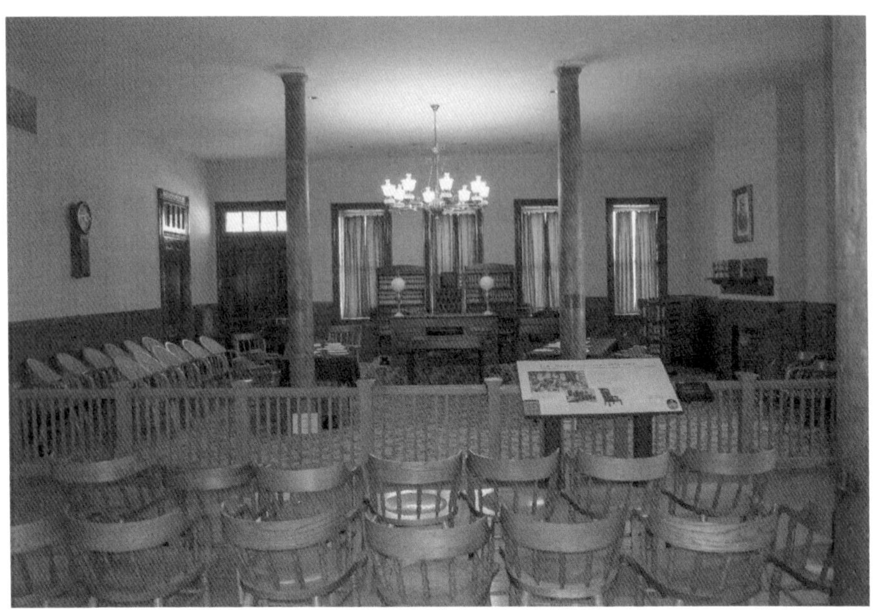

Restored courtroom of Judge Isaac Parker. Some original furnishings are located across the street at the history museum. *Photo by Bud Steed.*

The man never acknowledged her presence. He just kept his head down, appearing to read the book that lay open in front of him. He seemed to be completely ignoring her, so she asked again, a bit more forcefully this time, just who he was and what he was doing there. He continued to ignore her, which hacked her off (it would have me as well), so she walked right up to the railing and in a very loud voice asked him what he was doing there. She said the man straightened up at the desk, closed the book, let out a clearly audible heavy sigh, as if exasperated, and then slowly faded from sight. She said it was like he suddenly started to shimmer, turned transparent and then just faded completely from sight. Letting out a shriek, she turned and fled out of the room, running downstairs to the reception desk, where she blurted out the whole story to Linda, who had already had a few experiences of her own by then and who took it all in stride. Linda tried to get the poor woman to calm down, but she refused to go back upstairs without an escort. When she did get back into the courtroom, she did the fastest cleaning job that Linda had ever seen and then bolted for the door again. As for myself, I can't help but wonder who the man sitting at one of the lawyer's desk was. Could it have been the spirit of William H.H. Clayton, Judge Parker's prosecuting attorney? He was noted for putting in extremely long hours, as was Judge

Parker, so I guess it wouldn't be that far-fetched an assumption. Whoever he was, though, it was obvious that he didn't want to be disturbed.

In addition to the cleaning lady's experience, many other people have noted the sounds of footsteps in the courtroom, the smell of pipe tobacco, the sounds of muted conversation and rapping sounds as if a gavel were being struck on the desk, and one person even reported hearing what sounded like someone saying, "Excuse me please," in her ear as a cold breeze passed by her. All in all, there seems to be quite a bit of activity still going on in the courtroom.

The Museum Display

At the other end of the second floor, across from Judge Parker's courtroom, is the museum display. It contains educational displays about individuals who worked at or were tried in the courtroom; a section of old jail cells from the jail built and completed in 1888, complete with cot and iron bar doors; a hangman's noose; a gun alleged to have belonged to Cherokee Bill; and an assortment of handcuffs and manacles. It sheds light on the life of a prisoner and what some of them did to end up there, as well as on the man responsible for hanging them: George Maledon, the "Prince of Hangmen."

Most of the activity associated with the museum section of the second floor seems to revolve around shadows and voices. No one, to my knowledge, has ever seen an apparition in the museum section. Most people report hearing whispered voices and disembodied laughter, have the feeling of having their clothing and hair tugged on and catching the occasional movement of someone out of the corner of their eye—pretty normal stuff where ghosts and hauntings are associated.

One thing that a number of people have seen, though, is the shadowy form of a man wearing a hat. He seems to move from deep shadow to deep shadow, caught only as a fleeting glance by someone or seen peeking around the corner of a display or one of the jail cell walls. He doesn't interact with anyone and seems to prefer to remain hidden as much as possible—just watching and taking it all in. Those who have caught a quick glimpse of him have stated that they didn't get the feeling of any kind of dread or fear associated with him; in fact, they didn't feel anything at all associated with him. He just seems to be hanging around, not bothering anyone, and kind of gives off a vibe of peacefulness more than anything.

THE GALLOWS

The gallows, used to dispatch eighty-six souls to whatever awaited them on the other side of the veil, were at best a crude, though effective, method of execution and were in use from 1873 through 1896 in thirty-nine separate executions. The first gallows, erected in 1873, was placed near the stone wall of what was formerly the army's ammunition magazine (warehouse), and the executions held there from 1873 to 1876 were open to the public. Seven executions took place during that time, with a total of twenty-two men hanged by the neck until dead. It was eventually deemed that having the executions open to the public was not acceptable, so a sixteen-foot-high fence was erected around the gallows to keep the executions private. That took it from what could be called a public event, with people coming from miles around to witness the hangings, to become a private affair that saw fewer than fifty people in attendance at each execution.

The original gallows had a crossbeam from which the nooses were hung and a bench across the back for the prisoners to sit on while the sentence was read, but the last rebuilding of the gallows saw a slanted roof built over it. It had a huge sixteen-foot trapdoor, and the maximum capacity of men who could be hanged at the same time was most likely around eight, although legend has it that up to twelve men could be hanged at once. However, according to records, the most men to be hung at Fort Smith at one time was six, and that happened on two separate occasions. Anyone who took the walk up the twelve steps to the gallows floor was sure to meet their maker.

I found it interesting that while Judge Isaac Parker handed down 160 death sentences, out of that total only 79 men were actually hanged. Parker neither attended nor participated in the hangings in any way, and he was quite notably against the death penalty, preferring to place his faith in rehabilitation. Unfortunately, the law was clear, and anyone convicted on a charge of rape or murder was punished with death. Parker might not have been a fan of hanging a man, but the law was clear that he had to hand the sentence down anyway.

Today, the park service hangs the appropriate number of nooses on the gallows on the anniversary of each hanging that was carried out at Fort Smith. It's thought by some that the act of hanging those nooses on the crossbeam might be the trigger for some of the paranormal activity that is reported in the vicinity of the gallows.

One story that was told to me by Adam, the ranger I had talked to inside the visitors' center, concerned the hanging of the nooses on the crossbeam.

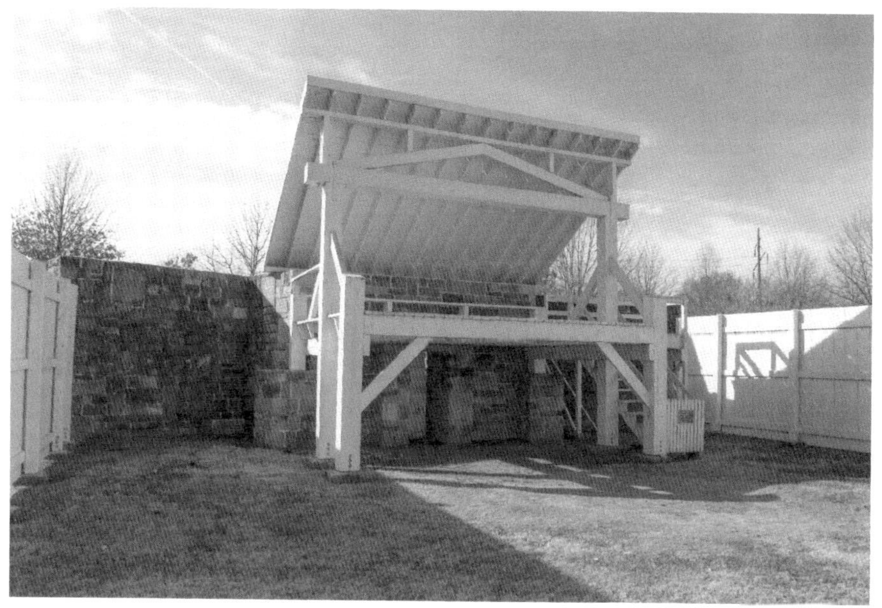

Replica of the gallows at Fort Smith. The original had been used to hang six men at one time earning Judge Parker's court the name of "Court of the Damned." *Photo by Bud Steed.*

They were hanging four nooses one morning, spacing them out evenly along the crossbeam. Just Adam and another ranger were taking care of it, tying off the loose end of the rope to the beam and letting about two feet of rope hanging down. It was a really quiet morning, kind of foggy and still out, and the other ranger had just tied off the second rope. Clear as a bell, they both heard a voice say, "You're doing it all wrong." They both just sort of stood there, as it was clear that the voice had come from up on the platform just a foot or two away from them; it was loud and it was close, and it was more than a little creepy. The other ranger looked first at Adam and then all around him as he said, "Sorry. We aren't professionals at this; we're just hanging up ropes." They both sort of chuckled about it, hurried up and hung the last ropes and quickly left the enclosure around the gallows. As they closed the door to the enclosure, they both looked up at the four ropes, and one of them in the middle was swinging back and forth in wide loops; the rest were hanging perfectly still. They just closed the door, latched it and walked quickly back to the visitors' center in silence. Adam said they both saw it happen, and after a few minutes of disbelief, they decided that it wasn't worth mentioning to anyone else. He thinks that it could have been the spirit of George Maledon, the "Prince of Hangmen," who made the comment on their obvious lack of skill where hanging nooses was concerned. He was a man who took a lot of pride in his job and liked things to be done perfectly.

Other people have reported hearing the sounds of conversation coming from inside the gallows enclosure. Whenever someone would check to see who was inside, the voices would stop, only to start up again as soon as the doors to the enclosure were shut. The sounds of footsteps on the gallows have been heard also, both on the steps and on the platform. One person reported seeing the apparition of a man in frontier clothing sitting on one of the steps, head bent down at an awkward angle; he was there one minute and then gone the next, vanishing into thin air.

During my second trip down to do a bit more research at the courthouse, I slipped inside the gallows enclosure to take a few additional photos for the book. I had an EMF meter, which measures electrical and magnetic fields to try and spot anomalies, in my coat pocket. I had been using it to quietly take readings inside the courthouse, kind of hiding it under my coat and hoping that no one would see me and say anything since officially they don't like paranormal investigations on the property. I did get a few interesting spikes inside the courtroom, but what really made

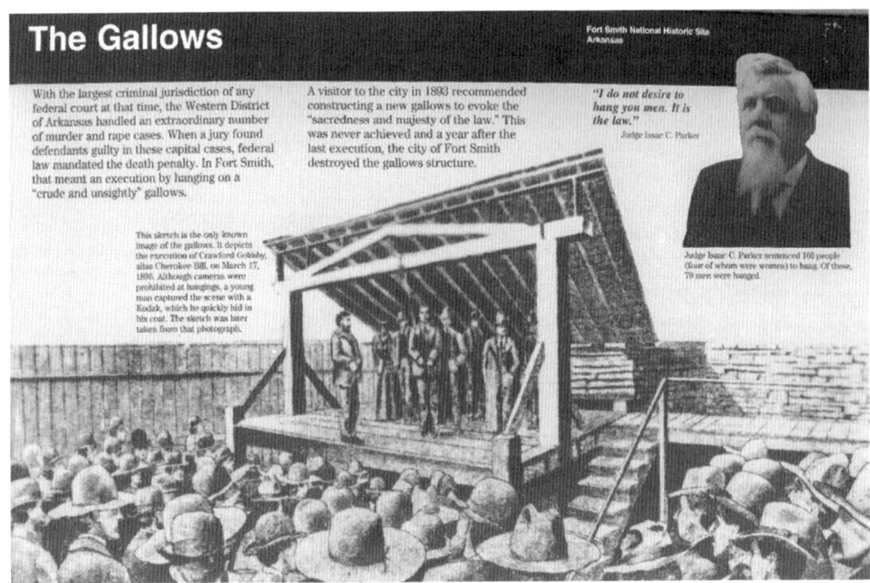

Plaque showing a sketch of the gallows during the hanging of Cherokee Bill. *Photo by Bud Steed.*

me take notice was the reading that I got inside the gallows enclosure. In an area with no electrical wiring overhead or close by, I should have been measuring 0 milligauss on the meter, especially outdoors, but that wasn't the case.

I was standing inside the enclosure just to the left of the display, which is a few steps inside, and to the left of the doorway. I pulled out the meter and started taking readings, which at first registered nothing at all. After I had been in there for a moment, I asked out loud if anyone was there and, if so, if they could do something to let me know they were there. I stood there for a few more minutes with nothing happening when it suddenly began to get colder—not a huge subzero drop in temperature or anything like that, but a noticeable drop nonetheless. At the same time, the meter came to life and started registering anywhere from 60 to 120 milligauss, which it certainly shouldn't have been doing. Outside like that, maybe a .02 or .04 fluctuation could be explained away, but not that much of a significant increase like the meter was displaying. I said, "Thank you for letting me know you are here. Could you let the meter drop back to zero?" A few moments later, it was registering zero.

I asked once again if they could move closer and change the numbers on the device in my hand; a moment later, it was registering between 60 and 120 milligauss once again. I repeated this a total of four times until I was interrupted by several tourists, who wanted to check out the gallows area. I sort of stood there like I was checking my e-mail on my cell phone, waiting for the people to leave. Once they were gone, I pulled the meter out and tried to pick up where I had left off. Unfortunately, I didn't get any additional spikes on the meter at all, and after about fifteen minutes of scanning with the meter and asking questions, I finally decided to leave. I have no explanation for the excessively high readings that I got on the meter or why they would go away and then come back almost on command when I asked them to. Is it possible that a spirit was manipulating the meter to let me know that it was there? Certainly. I like to think that was exactly what had happened, but the skeptic in me still feels the need to find a logical answer. Such an answer could be obtained only if a team or even a single paranormal investigator were allowed to do a proper investigation of the property. I can't help but think that there are several souls hanging around the property that have something they want to say.

The Commissary Building

Fort Smith's oldest standing building, the commissary, was built between 1838 and 1846 as a storehouse for military supplies. It also served as a supply depot from which supplies were sent during the Mexican-American War, which was fought from 1846 to 1848. From 1875 to 1890, Judge Isaac Parker used part of the second floor as his office, and some people speculate that it is his spirit that is seen both looking out the second-floor window and walking across the grass from the courthouse toward the commissary. The lower floor was used as housing for various court personnel, although today it is outfitted much as it would have been during its days as a supply warehouse. The building fell into a state of disrepair and was eventually scheduled for demolition, but it was rescued in 1909. From 1910 all the way to 1979, it served as the city's first history museum.

While visiting the current history museum, I spoke with a very nice lady who told me that she used to work over at the commissary building when it was the museum. She stated that she had experienced the apparition of a man in a dark suit while on the second floor. He was an older man wearing a high-collar white shirt buttoned all the way to the top and had on a pair of suspenders; his black coat was draped over his arm. It was early morning before they opened up, and she was getting things ready for the day to kick off when she happened to glance up and see him standing there, looking at her. A bit surprised and feeling a little alarmed, she started to tell him that they weren't open yet and to ask him how he got in (the door was locked from the inside), but then she noticed that from the knees down there was nothing there—no pants, no shoes, just empty space. She said she straightened up all the way very quickly and let out a little shriek. As she stood there, hand over her mouth, just looking at him, he simply faded away. Shaken up by what she had just seen, she backed up a few steps and sat down, unsure of what to do next. As she sat there, replaying it over in her head, she realized that she never felt threatened at all—the man had just seemed a bit curious—so she decided that it really wasn't anything to get worked up about. Regaining her composure, she went back to work, although she did keep an eye out for anything else strange that might happen. When she told her coworkers what she had experienced, she was initially afraid that they would think she was crazy, but to her surprise, they all had a story or two about something they had experienced. One other person had even seen the same man walking across the upstairs floor one morning.

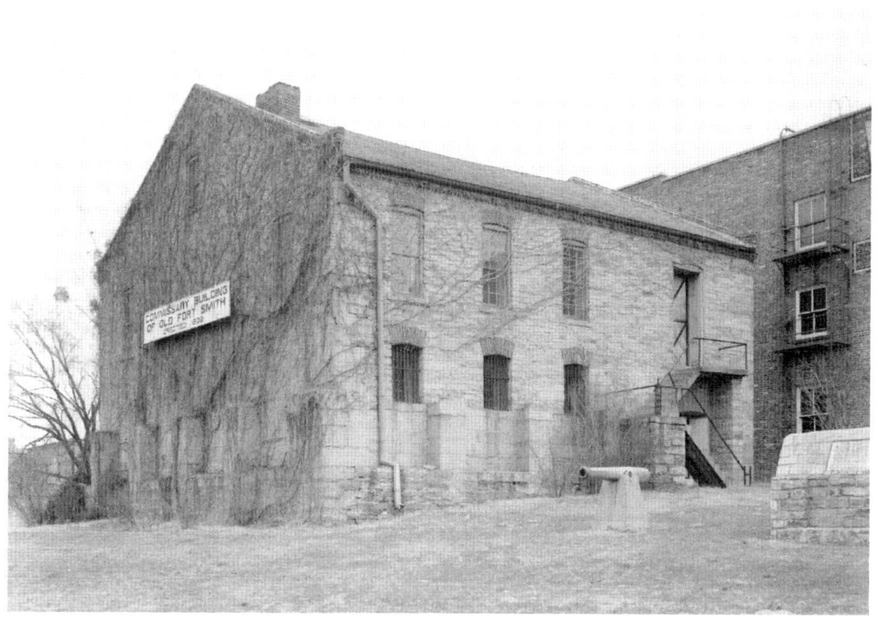

The commissary building in 1940. *Courtesy of the Library of Congress.*

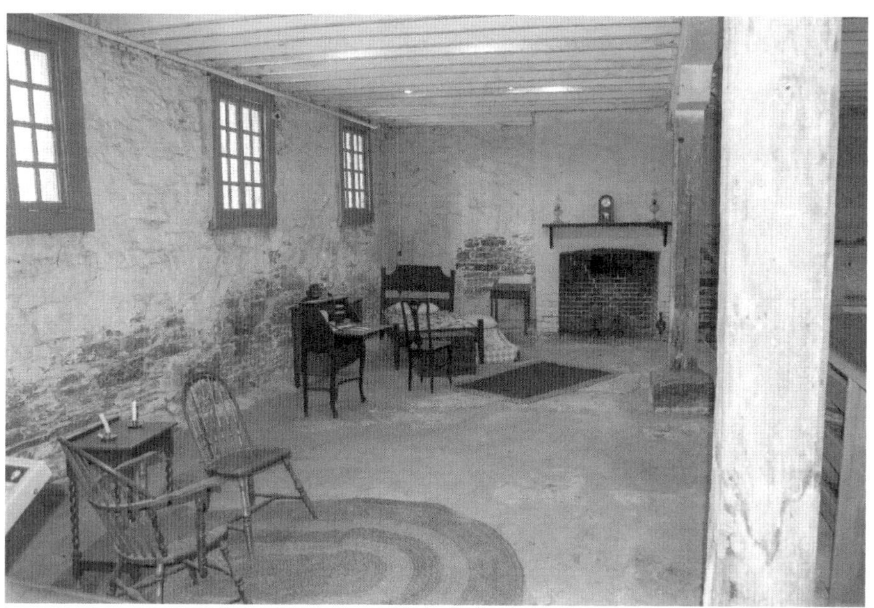

A view of the interior of the commissary building as it might have looked when it was used as housing for court officials. *Photo by Bud Steed.*

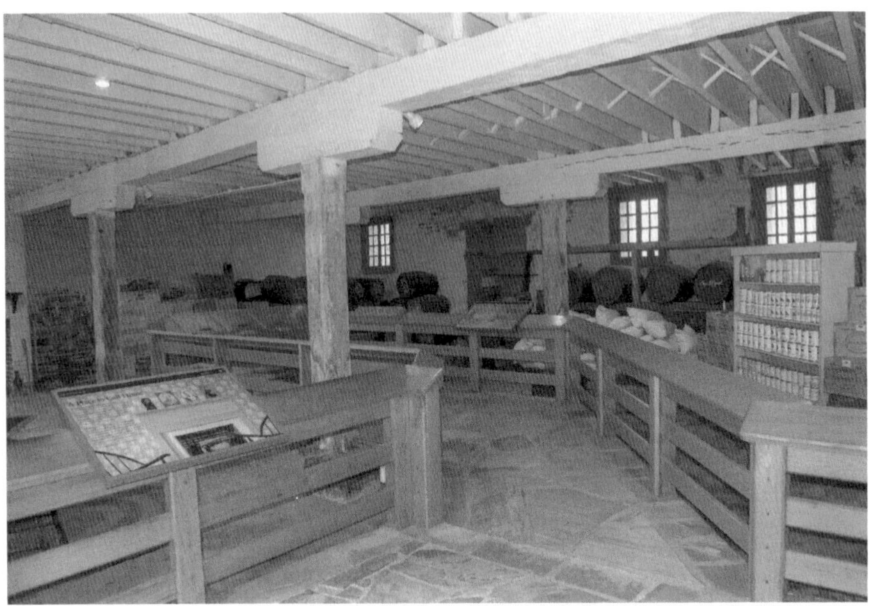

The inside of the commissary building as it might have looked when it held supplies for the fort. *Photo by Bud Steed.*

She told me that later on, she would hear footsteps and voices throughout the building and that she started referring to the man in the suit as Henry for some reason, although she didn't really know why. When she would open up, she would say, "Good morning, Mr. Henry" as she opened the door, and she confided that she came to think of him as just another co-worker. Exactly who he was or why he was hanging around the building was never determined. She also told me that since they moved to their current location, she has never seen him again. That would lead me to believe that he wasn't attached to something that the museum owns but that he might be attached to or just lingering around the building itself for some reason.

The fact that she saw nothing from the knees down on the apparition isn't really that unusual either. There are many accounts of people seeing spirits that have no lower legs and, in some cases, nothing from the waist down. My theory is that it takes an enormous amount of energy for a spirit to manifest and that it might be just a bit too much for them to manage with the energy they have to get the entire body to show up. Like I said, it's just a theory, and I have no facts with which to back it up, but for some reason or other, there are an awful lot of accounts of spirits missing parts of their bodies.

THE PARK GROUNDS

Looking at the grounds around the courthouse and commissary, as well as the walking trails down to the old fort site, it's easy to forget that this was once a working military fort. Numerous buildings and quarters, stables, parade grounds and everything else that once came with an army fort dotted the landscape around the old courthouse and down to the river at Belle Point. It's not easy to imagine how it once looked. But even though very little remains of the second fort and even less of the original, from time to time things seem to happen that remind park visitors that things weren't always as peaceful as they are now.

The sounds of conversation, laughter and the shouts of men are heard wafting across the open expanse of ground between the commissary and the courthouse, even though no one is anywhere close around. The sounds of horses moving and men marching as if on drill are often heard as well, with several reports claiming that it sounded as if several men were running at top speed past them. My son Sean and I experienced something similar to that at the Prairie Grove Battlefield when we were researching my book *Haunted Northwest Arkansas*.

One of the oddest stories that I came across, and one that was similar to a story that I heard while in Baton Rouge, Louisiana, was told to me by a gentleman named Jim, whom I met at the Fort Smith National Cemetery close by. He told me that he often walks on the trails in the park area in the evening hours as a way to get a little exercise when the weather's nice. It was summer, and the weather was perfect when he had his experience. The sun was just starting to set, there was a bit of breeze to help cool things off and there didn't seem to be a soul around on the walking trails to bother him. He was walking on the path that runs between the courthouse and the commissary and away from the buildings. He said he started to faintly hear what sounded like men talking and several horses walking coming from behind him. He glanced back over his shoulder, but there was nothing anywhere close to him. He shrugged it off and kept walking, but it started to get louder and louder. Nervously, he turned to look behind him once again, but this time, instead of just open space, he saw a group of five men walking along, each of them leading a saddled horse, just a short distance behind him and to his left.

They were dressed in uniform, what he assumed were old army uniforms or cavalry uniforms, and were simply walking along talking. Jim had no idea where they had come from, as there was nothing but open space all around him and nothing had been visible before. As they got close to where he was standing, he remembered the creak of the saddles, the sounds of the horses and even the smell of the horses. For a moment, he thought maybe they might be reenactors getting ready to go home or something. The men and horses passed within a few feet of Jim, and as he turned to watch them walk by, he noted that neither the men nor the horses seemed to be aware of him at all—no eye contact, no nod of the head or a simple greeting, nothing at all. It was as if they didn't even know he existed. As he watched the men and horses move on across the grass, they started to take on almost a glow of sorts, like they were all lit up around the edges. They then began to flicker and fade. As he watched, there was a sudden burst of light around them, like someone flashed a super-bright flashlight right in the middle of them, and then they were gone. There were no more sounds of horses, no conversation—just silence once again. He said he walked over to where he had seen them disappear, but there was nothing there at all. No tracks or anything of the kind to show that they were ever there. Obviously puzzled by what he had just seen, he walked back over to the path and sat down on the ground to think it through. After about twenty minutes of going over it in his head, replaying the whole thing from start to finish in his mind, Jim said he came to the conclusion that there just wasn't any logical or rational explanation for it. He is convinced that what he saw was a group of ghostly soldiers walking their horses—nothing more, nothing less.

As for my thoughts on what he saw, it has all the hallmarks of a residual haunting. The spirits don't seem to be aware of anything outside of what they are doing. They appeared for a moment and then disappeared, and there were smells and sounds associated with it. The only wrinkle in it is that I can't find any other account of anyone other than Jim having observed this particular event. Also, in most residual haunting cases, there is usually some traumatic incident or emotional trauma that set the event in motion. Several soldiers walking their horses doesn't seem to fit the "emotional trauma" theory at all.

As for Jim, he still walks the trails around the old fort and the courthouse, enjoying his walks and the fresh air, but he also keeps an eye out for anything unusual that might suddenly appear—horses, men or something else entirely. A part of him hopes to see something else around the old fort again. He said that it was one of the most fascinating experiences he's ever had.

In addition to Jim's experience, others have caught brief glimpses of soldiers walking on the grounds, as well as shadow figures that seem to appear momentarily from behind a tree or are seen peeking around the corner of a building. The park grounds around the commissary and the old courthouse seem to have a lot of paranormal activity associated with them. It's a shame they can't be formally investigated. I think they would produce some very interesting evidence.

The Old Fort at Belle Point

At the site of the original fort, the only thing that still remains of it is a stone building foundation, a few memorial and educational plaques, an iron ring embedded in the rock at the river's edge used for tying off supply boats and the lonely spirit of a man that roams the old fort area and seems to be searching for something. I've heard several accounts of this spirit, and they all run pretty much the same. He's seen walking the old fort grounds and along the river's edge, scanning the ground in front of him and occasionally stopping to bend down and look at, or for, something on the ground. After a few moments, he straightens up, obviously agitated, and he starts the whole thing over again.

Those who have seen him say that he is dressed in what looks to be an old-fashioned military uniform: light-colored pants with a stripe down the leg; a dark coat that is rather long, hitting him about halfway from the waist to the knee; a wide belt of some type around his waist; and a strap that crosses from his shoulder down to the belt. They say that he is a younger-looking fellow with long sideburns and closely cropped hair and is of average build and height. Who he is or why he is obviously searching for something has never been determined. Those who have seen him say that when he is approached he just disappears, only to reappear a short distance away, still intent on finding something. That he doesn't want to be bothered is pretty clear.

Along with the searching man, there have been reports of voices singing and the sounds of people moving about. One person claims to have seen the figure of a soldier materialize inside the ruins of the foundation, walk up the step to the ground, take a few steps across the grass and then disappear. But one of the coolest reports that I have come across—and I was lucky enough to actually hear it from the person who experienced it—was that of the pipe-smoking man.

Janet is a native of Fort Smith and frequents the old fort area and the walking trails. She says she likes to walk down by the old fort foundation and just sit for a while, watching the river and taking in the sounds around her.

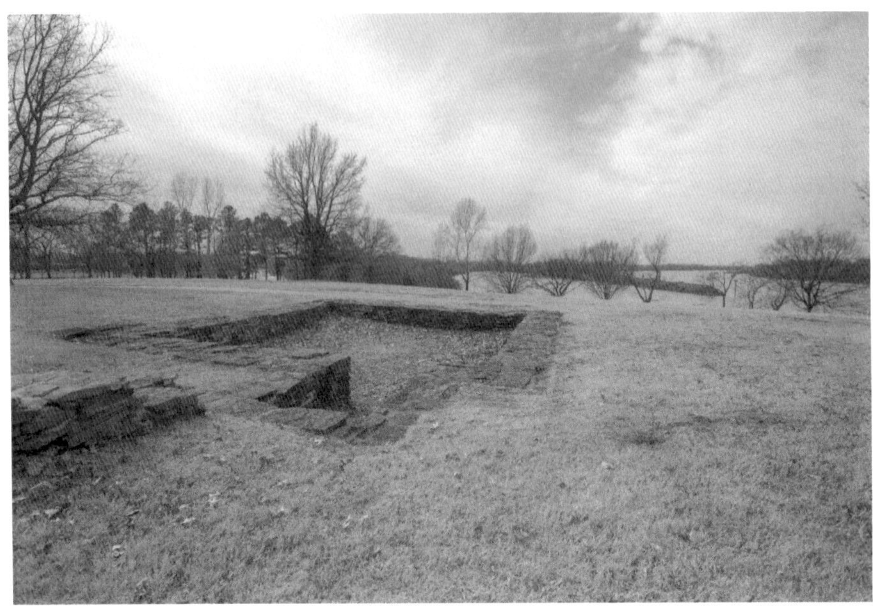

The stone foundations of one of the original old Fort Smith buildings at Belle Point. *Photo by Adrian Scalf.*

On one particular occasion, she was down by the old fort area in the early morning hours, and she said it was an absolutely beautiful morning—warm, sunny, not a bit of breeze, just a quiet and perfect morning to be outside. She sat down on the grass a little ways in front of the old stone foundation and settled back to watch the river. She said that she had only been there for a few moments when she heard a man's voice come from her right. He said something to the effect of, "Good morning, madam. A beautiful day, is it not?" Janet said she almost jumped two feet off the ground she was so startled. She whipped her head to the right and saw an older-looking gentleman sitting on the grass a few feet away from her smoking a pipe. As might be expected, Janet told him that he had startled her, and he apologized. She said that they sat there for a few moments exchanging pleasantries when it suddenly occurred to her that she wasn't smelling his pipe tobacco at all. And then she realized that she hadn't seen him sitting there, nor heard him approach, even though it was a pretty open area, with just a few trees spread out in a parklike setting.

Janet remarked that she hadn't seen him when she came up, to which the man chuckled and said, "Not many people seem to take notice of me anymore." Then he went back to smoking his pipe, gazing out at the river as if suddenly lost in thought. Starting to get a little unnerved, Janet turned back away for a moment and fidgeted with her bag, getting ready to make an excuse in order to vacate the premises. As she turned back around to tell the man that she had forgotten something in her car and to wish him a good day, he was no longer there. Janet jumped to her feet and looked all around, but the man was nowhere to be seen. Where they were sitting, it was impossible for the man to hide or get out of sight in the moment that she had turned away. Thoroughly shaken up now, she grabbed her bag and hurried back to her car, glancing behind her from time to time but not finding anyone or anything there at all. Janet told me that she sat in her car for a few moments, calming herself down, and realized that she was being silly. She didn't have any doubt at all that she had just seen a ghost, as there really wasn't any other explanation for it; a person just doesn't get out of sight that quickly. She also realized that she never really felt threatened at all, even when she was surprised at the sound of his voice. He had seemed the perfect gentleman and was just interested in the same thing that she was: relaxing for a bit, watching the river and enjoying the day. Janet admitted to being a bit nervous the next several times that she went there, not really knowing if she would see him again or not. A part

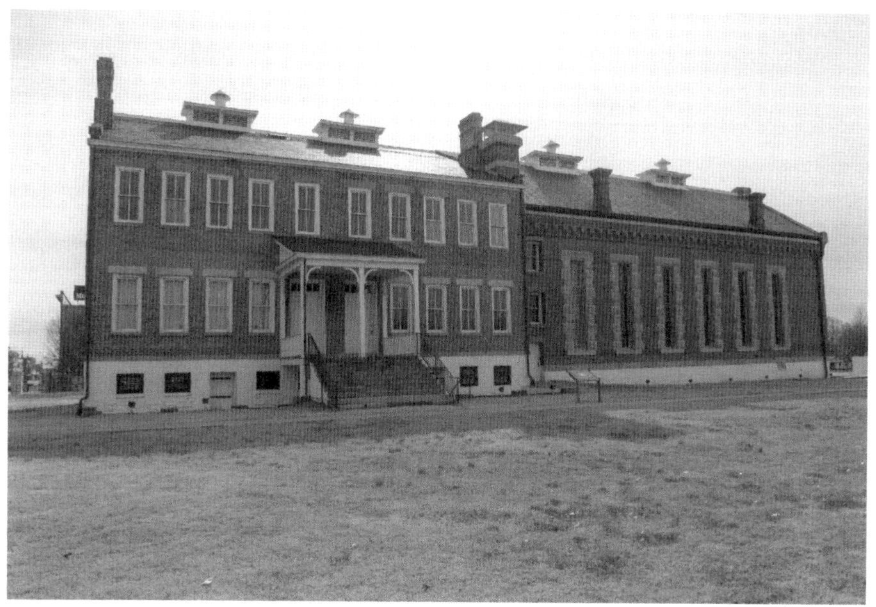

Another view of the historic Fort Smith Courthouse. *Photo by Bud Steed.*

of her hoped that she would. She has smelled pipe tobacco from time to time though, even though she is the only person anywhere close around. She says that when she smells it, she just says, "Good morning," comments about what a fine day it is and then settles back to watch the river. So far, no one has ever returned the greeting.

The old fort and the entire park area around the old courthouse seem to have an unusual amount of activity associated with them, even though you don't hear a lot about it. Most of the park workers are hesitant to discuss it because the official stance is that nothing haunts the place at all. The unofficial consensus seems to be that not only is the place haunted, it's actually haunted by quite a lot of entities and in just about every area and building.

My hope is that someday we might be allowed access to investigate the entire park grounds as well as the buildings to see if some type of evidence might be documented. It took me six months of inquiries and paperwork to finally be granted access to do an overnight investigation of Wilson's Creek National Battlefield, so I still have hope that someday we will get to investigate the old commissary building and the courthouse. If we do, I'll be sure to post whatever findings we get on my Backroads Paranormal website and on the Backroads Paranormal Facebook page (facebook.com/BackroadsParanormal) for all of you to check out. Wish me luck on getting access!

Fort Smith National Cemetery

Situated a short distance from the grounds of the old courthouse and the old fort, the Fort Smith National Cemetery is the final resting place for a large number of America's finest and their spouses. Established sometime around 1838, when the army returned to rebuild Fort Smith and elevated to a National Cemetery to be directed by the War Department by President Grant in 1871 after the military post was closed, the burial ground itself probably dates back to about 1819, when the post surgeon, Thomas Russell, died. In 1823, fifty men assigned to the post died, forty-four of those deaths taking place over the course of the summer months—accidents, disease and likely poor living conditions contributed to those deaths, but I was not able to locate much in the way of death records.

During the Confederate occupation of the fort from 1861, until it was taken by Union troops in 1863, the Confederates utilized the cemetery. An estimated four hundred Confederate troops were buried there over the course of the war. It should be noted though that some of those buried there were killed in other battles and reinterred in the cemetery after the war had ended and that not all were killed in the Fort Smith area. By 1867, the cemetery consisted of five acres surrounded by a whitewashed fence, and over the course of time, it has expanded to the thirty-two-acre site that you see today.

Many notables are buried here, including "Hanging Judge" Isaac Parker and Fort Smith native Brigadier General William O. Darby, who formed and commanded "Darby's Rangers," the First Ranger Battalion, which fought

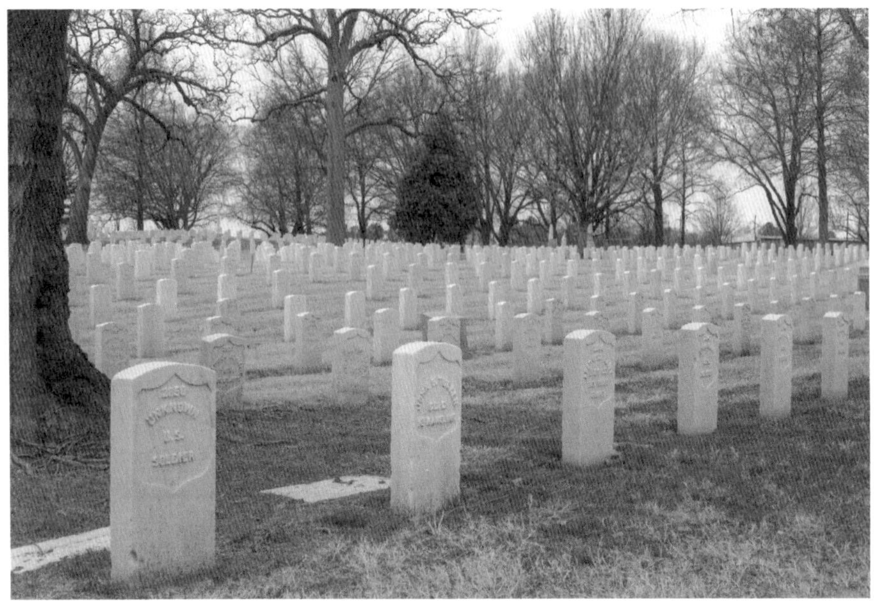

Civil War headstones at the Fort Smith National Cemetery. *Photo by Bud Steed.*

in World War II. More than thirteen thousand service men and women, along with their spouses, are buried at the national cemetery today, and the number continues to grow.

One interesting thing that I found on the U.S. Department of Veterans Affairs website was that the government-issued headstones face east, while many of the privately furnished headstones face west. As in most Christian burials, the body is placed with the head in the west and the feet in the east so that when they rise from the grave at the coming of Christ, they are facing his direction. While I was familiar with this custom, I had no idea that the reason for the headstone to face west was so that a person who was reading it would be in the proper position (facing east as in the coming of Christ) to say a prayer for them. The website states that it is a local Arkansas custom, but after reflecting on it for a bit, I realized that most cemeteries that I have been in are set up the same way. I had simply never realized it before.

A number of paranormal occurrences have been noted in the cemetery over the years, with most of them consisting of disembodied voices, people being touched, clothing and hair being pulled and the occasional apparition—the usual smorgasbord of paranormal activity—but one recurring incident seems to come to the forefront. This particular report isn't unusual at all, and I have heard it told about almost every military cemetery that I have been in or researched whether Union, Confederate or otherwise: the Civil War–era ghost soldier that appears to be on guard duty, protecting the remains of his fallen comrades-in-arms. This apparition is alleged to be seen mostly at night, although in a few instances it has been seen in the daylight hours, walking a recurring path among the headstones and along the perimeter. The apparition associated with the Fort Smith National Cemetery seems to be performing the same duty, diligently roaming the area on eternal watch over his comrades. One person who has seen him said that he seems to watch things pretty closely.

The Soldier on Duty

The area around the cemetery isn't really what you would call a neighborhood like those surrounding some cemeteries. The downtown area is just a few blocks away, the old fort and courthouse are close by and a warehouse of sorts sits behind it. Basically, you need a reason to be down there; you just don't look out your kitchen window into the graveyard. So, when I run across a story of someone who has witnessed something in a cemetery like the one in Fort Smith, I naturally have to wonder what they were doing there in the first place. Most people have a reasonable explanation, such as driving by on their way to work or out taking a walk, but Dana, who related this story to me, had a different reason for being there: she likes photographing cemeteries in the dark. Not the strangest hobby I've ever run across, but it is in the top ten.

Now, the cemetery is only open from 0700 to sunset each day for visitors, but apparently, trespassing laws mean little to Dana. In her own words, "I'm not really bothering anything or anyone, and it's really easy to get in and out of the place with no one noticing you, so I don't really see a problem with it. It's not like I'm vandalizing anything—I'm just taking photographs." While I can understand her logic, I don't recommend that anyone doing photography or a paranormal investigation or whatever do so without obtaining permission to be on the property you are investigating or taking photos of. Cops have a dim view of people lurking about closed cemeteries in the dark, and the last thing anyone needs to be accused of is being a grave robber, so just don't do it, okay?

But anyway, Dana was in the cemetery on a full moon night at about 0200. She has black hair and likes to dress in black, sort of a Goth look I suppose you could say, so she was blending in pretty well in the shadows, moving quietly from tree to tree in the Civil War section of the cemetery. She had a tripod with her camera mounted on it along with a remote to control the shutter and was just setting up here and there, taking long exposures using the moonlight for available light.

She was moving out into one of the cemetery roads to take a photo of all of the gravestones lined up in a perfect row when she heard someone behind her say, "You are not supposed to be here." Figuring that she had just been busted, she turned around, thinking she was going to see a police officer or two standing there, but to her surprise, no one was there. She thought that maybe she had imagined it, so she turned back around to continue setting up her shot. It wasn't the first time something strange had happened to her while she was taking photos at night in a cemetery. She had finished setting up and clicked off a few shots when she felt a hand on her shoulder and heard the same voice say, "I told you. You are not supposed to be here, now git!" Dana admitted that she jumped forward about two feet when it happened, nearly knocking over her camera, and spun around to confront whoever it was. Once again, no one was anywhere close around; the night was bright, clear and silent, and Dana was admittedly more than a little freaked out.

As she gathered up her camera gear, she said, "Okay, okay, I'm leaving. I didn't mean to upset anyone." She started moving up the road toward the back wall, and after about twenty yards or so, she stopped and glanced behind her to where she had just been taking photos. She swears that standing in the road in the full moonlight was a Civil War soldier watching her leave. She thought about stopping to see if she could get a photo but thought the better of it; he seemed pretty intent on her leaving, so instead, she simply waved at him. To her surprise, the soldier raised a hand as if in goodbye and then faded from sight. Dana said she wasted no time at all in turning tail and getting out of the cemetery.

When I asked her if her experience had changed her attitude about photographing cemeteries at night, she told me that she still continues to do so, but she now periodically says out loud, "I'm not here to bother you or anything else; I'm just taking photos. Give me a few minutes, and I'll move on." She said she isn't sure if it works or not, but she hasn't been ordered away from anywhere since.

Cemetery Lights

Another unusual story (one I've only run across one other time) is associated with the Fayetteville National Cemetery in Fayetteville, Arkansas, and concerns moving lights. The lights at the Fort Smith National Cemetery are seen in the early hours of the morning, are blue in color and seem to follow a path among the headstones. Sometimes they move together as if following one another, and at other times they split off and travel a distance on their own. When one of the lights gets to a particular headstone, it changes from blue to a bright white and then drops down to the ground, disappearing from sight. It's always interesting to run across someone who has allegedly witnessed it firsthand.

Daryl, a young man I spoke with while taking photos of the cemetery, told me that he has seen the lights on multiple occasions. He likes to run and finds that the trails around the courthouse and old fort areas, along with the roads around the cemetery, are a great place to get his exercise in. As a paralegal for a local attorney, he puts in really long hours and finds that running in the early morning hours, sometimes even in the dark, best suits his schedule.

One morning, around 0500, he was out for a run in the dark and was passing the cemetery when he noticed about half a dozen balls of bright-blue light moving around; he estimated them to be about three feet off the ground, and they seemed to hold a steady height, with little up or down fluctuation. They were moving in a uniform pattern among the headstones, pausing for a moment and then continuing on. Slightly bewildered, he stopped and stood there watching them, looking for some telltale stream of light that might lead him to the source of the lights, but he simply couldn't locate any. There didn't seem to be anyone with a flashlight, laser pointer or something else anywhere near the lights at all; they seemed to be their own source of illumination.

As he watched, some of the lights would split off from the group, going their own way for a bit and then rejoin the group as they weaved among the headstones. He stated that every so often, one of the lights would pause at a headstone, change to an almost blinding white light and then drop down to the ground and disappear. He watched until there was only one light remaining, weaving among the headstones near the fence where he was standing. It suddenly changed direction and came straight toward where he was at. To his amazement, it stopped on the other side of the fence directly across from him. He said it was fluid-like, changing shape, pulsating and changing color from a light blue to a dark blue; the air had an almost electric

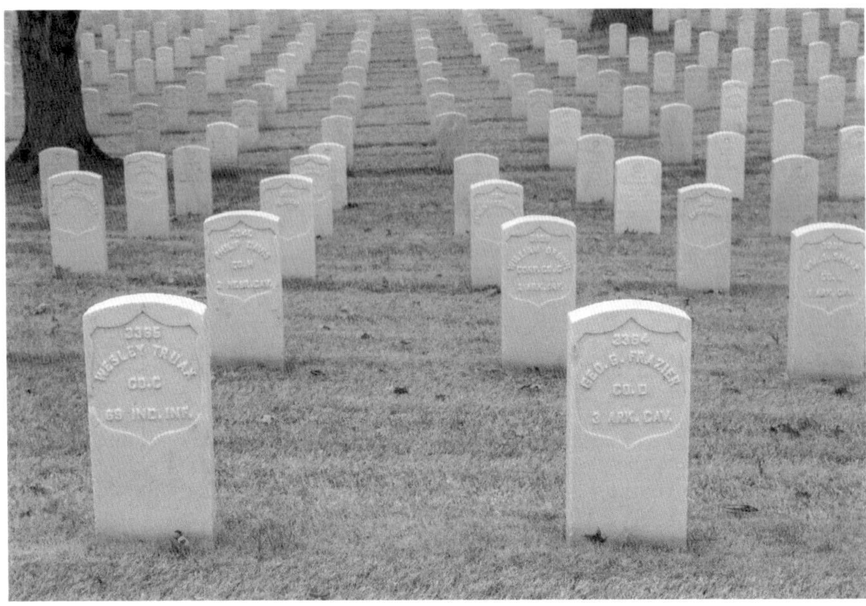

Grave markers at the Fort Smith National Cemetery. *Photo by Bud Steed.*

charge to it, and he said he could feel the hair on his arms and neck standing on end. After a few minutes of it just hovering there in front of him, it slowly moved off among the headstones until it, like the others, changed to a bright white light and then disappeared into the ground.

He really didn't know what to make of it; try as he might, he hasn't been able to come up with a logical explanation for what he witnessed that time or the other times. So far, he has seen the "cemetery lights," as he likes to refer to them, about seven different times—always in the same cemetery section, about the same time of the morning each time and only when he has been out running. He drove over there several times to see if he might be able to get a photo from his car, just to prove to people that he wasn't crazy, but even after parking close by and waiting for more than an hour, he failed to see anything at all, except for a police officer who told him to move along after running his license; it only seems to happen when he is outside by himself.

Daryl said that he has never felt scared or nervous, even when it was directly across the fence from him. He believes that the lights are some kind of paranormal activity, most likely a spirit, and the light is just the shape that they take when moving about. He still runs in the same area each week, but

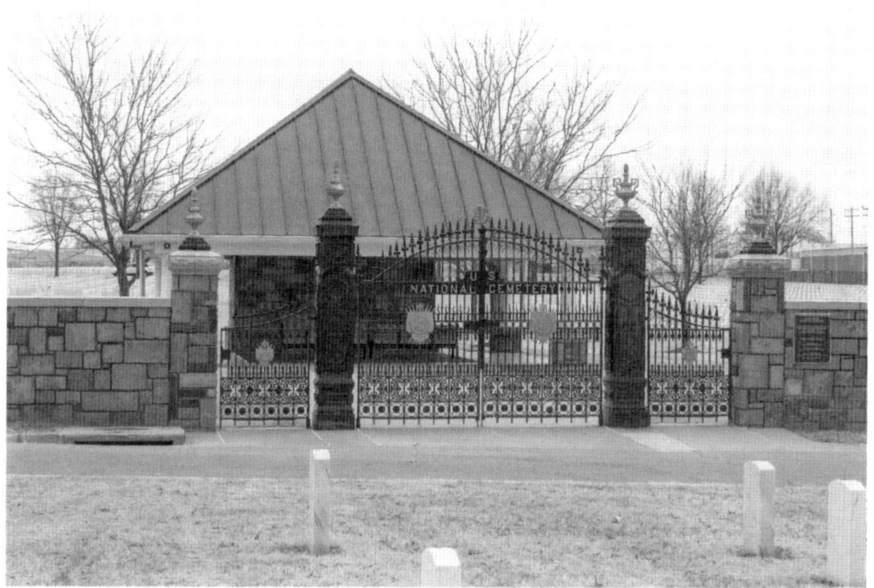

Gates to the pavilion at the Fort Smith National Cemetery. *Photo by Bud Steed.*

now he doesn't even bother to look for the lights—if they are there, that's cool; if not, that's cool too. He figures that if they don't bother him, he won't bother them and everyone will end up happy. It's too bad that more people, alive or dead, can't develop the same philosophy.

It seems as if there are tons of stories associated with cemeteries, although in all honesty, I've never figured out why. I've witnessed some strange things myself while visiting cemeteries all over the country, most specifically at the Natchez City Cemetery in Natchez, Mississippi, a place with an unusual amount of activity. I wrote about it in the *Haunted Natchez Trace*, and if you are able, you should take a trip down there and check it out. It's quite a remarkable place. I can't help but wonder why a spirit would remain in or haunt a cemetery. Is there some sort of attachment to their mortal remains, some comfort to them knowing where they are buried, or is it something else entirely? I imagine that if necessary, I could certainly find a better place to haunt than a cemetery, yet there are tons of reports of paranormal activity associated with them, and the Fort Smith National Cemetery is no exception.

Fort Smith Museum of History

Probably the coolest place in Fort Smith, from my perspective, is the Fort Smith Museum of History. I mean, it has a working soda fountain that serves real ice cream sodas and sundaes! It's like stepping back in time when the local pharmacy had a soda fountain and lunch counters were where everyone stopped for a quick bite to eat—simpler times without the Internet and GPS tracking devices, and people had a level of pride in themselves and what they did. But I digress.

Located at 320 Rogers Avenue in the historic Atkinson-Williams Warehouse, the museum holds more than forty thousand artifacts directly related to Fort Smith and the surrounding areas' history. Originally formed in 1910 to save the old commissary building from destruction, it was housed there until 1979 when it moved into its current location. The Atkinson-Williams building is listed in the National Register of Historic Places, quite a fitting location for a history museum.

Permanent exhibits on the first floor show the progression of Fort Smith's growth and development, and the second floor holds an exhibition titled "In the Shadows of the Gallows" that has furnishings from Judge Parker's courtroom. Other exhibits, like in the William O. Darby Memorial Room, help to showcase prominent Fort Smith natives, as well as depict what life was like in Fort Smith. Another section of the museum, the Boyd Gallery, hosts traveling and temporary displays, with a lot of the items being placed from the vast stock of artifacts that the museum maintains. Sadly, the museum doesn't allow photographs to be taken for commercial use, of which inclusion

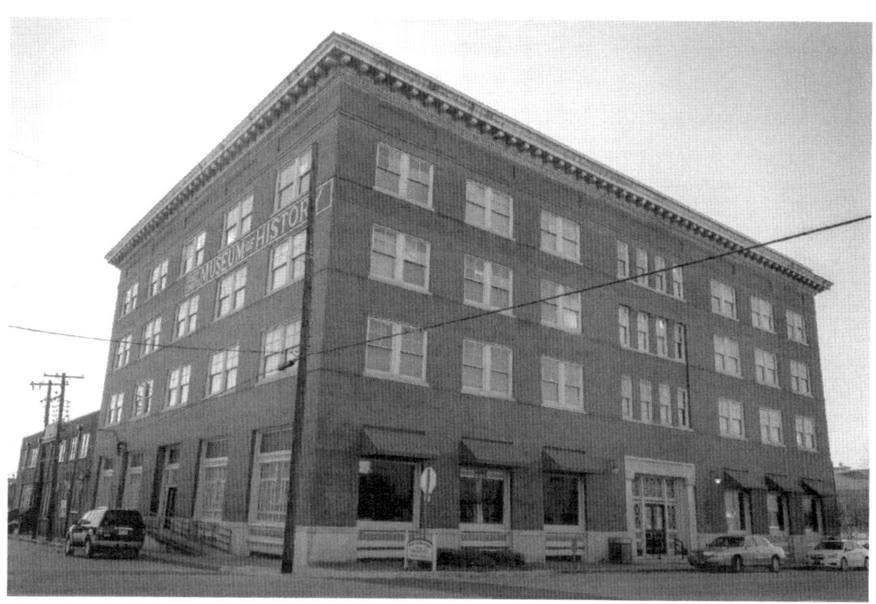

Exterior view of the Fort Smith Museum of History. The second floor is where the woman is seen looking out of the window. *Photo by Adrian Scalf.*

in this book would be considered, so I wasn't able to take any images of the interior of the building or the exhibits. They do allow photos to be taken for private use, although flash photography is never allowed, so keep that in mind if you ever decide to visit. Despite the photography restrictions, it's a very cool educational facility; it's also a very haunted facility.

There have been numerous reports over the years of paranormal activity, everything from apparitions to disembodied voices to people being touched—the whole gamut of the usual supernatural occurrences that one associates with haunted locations. With the huge number of artifacts owned and maintained by the museum and the possibility of spirit attachments to objects, it's little wonder that reports of activity abound here. Oddly enough, there seems to be a spirit that hangs around outside the rear of the building as well.

The Warehouse Worker

Often seen around the rear of the history museum building, the spirit, which is sometimes referred to as the "warehouse worker" and at other times as the "loafer"—two names that seem a bit contradictory—is sometimes seen going through the motions of working at some task or another, yet at other times it's simply lounging on the ground, leaning back against something that doesn't seem to be there. At first, I thought that perhaps there were two different spirits being mentioned, but after comparing the descriptions of him from several different accounts, it would appear that it is the same man.

Said to be a tall, thin man in his late twenties or early thirties and dressed in the work clothes of someone from the '30s or '40s, he is seen only briefly before disappearing, and as far as I have been able to determine, no one has ever had an interaction with him. Anyone who has ever seen him and tried to approach him or call out to him have stated that he doesn't seem to want to interact; he just disappears.

At first, I thought that maybe he was simply a residual type of haunting. I've run across this phenomenon quite a few times, one really good example being the man at the Pirate House property in Waveland, Mississippi, that I documented in my *Haunted Mississippi Gulf Coast* book. He's seen going through the motions of chopping wood before he disappears, much like the warehouse worker. However, where a residual haunting has no awareness, this alleged spirit seems to be aware. In several of the accounts, he will raise his head from his task or turn to look at whoever called out to him before disappearing. This would suggest to me that he is aware and intelligent—he just doesn't want to be messed with. But I'm still bothered by the fact that he seems to be going about some unseen task during the times when he is seen working. By the accounts that I've heard, he seems to be bent over as if working on something, doing the same task again and again before disappearing, but no one has ever seen what it is he is working on.

While I've heard this story about the worker from several different people over the years, and I have no reason to doubt that what they tell me is what they saw or think they saw, for me, the verdict is still out on this one. While I don't know everything about the paranormal (and you should be extremely careful of those who claim they do), this story contains elements of both a residual and intelligent haunting, and I've never run across an accurate story that had both. I'm afraid that in this case, I'll have to leave it up to you to decide if you think it is a true ghost sighting or just an urban legend.

The Lady in the Window

Another alleged spirit sighting is that of the lady in the window. Usually seen in the evenings and early morning hours, either before the museum opens or after everyone has gone home, the image of a woman in a high-collar dress with her hair piled neatly on top of her head in a bun, is seen standing in the second-floor window looking out at the street. She has been described as being a middle-aged woman, rather good looking from a distance, and she seems to be watching out the window. Whether she is simply watching people and traffic go by or if she is watching for someone is unknown, as is who she might actually be. She can be seen from outside moving from window to window sometimes, as if she is just walking around the second floor, pausing from time to time to look out the window.

Since the place used to be a hardware and a warehouse, it would seem unlikely that the woman might have spent a lot of time there—not impossible but unlikely—so my thoughts are that she could quite possibly be attached to some artifact that the museum has in its possession. Several people have heard a woman's voice, soft and low, on the second floor, as well as the sounds of soft humming and singing. While there is no way to tell for certain, it could be the same woman. While two female spirits occupying the

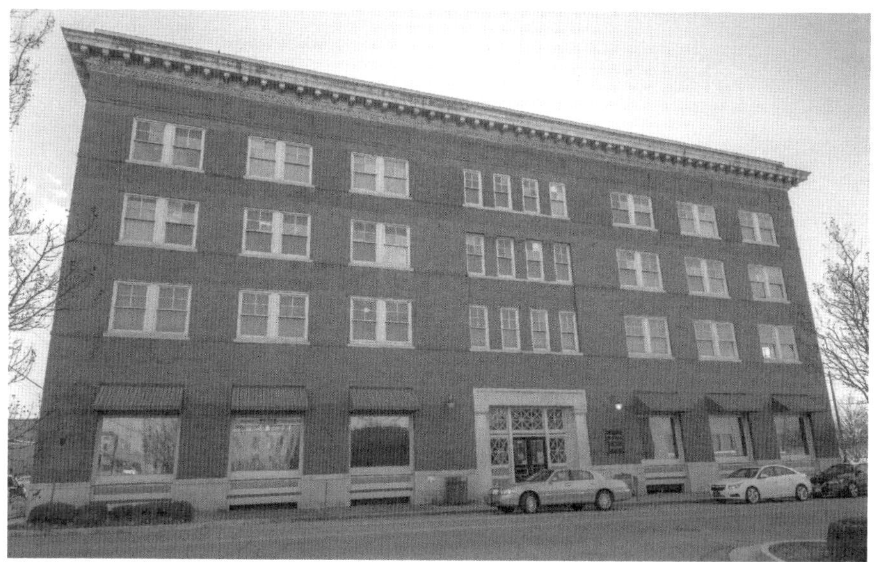

Front view of the Fort Smith Museum of History. *Photo by Adrian Scalf.*

same building might not be that strange, two occupying the second floor of what used to be a hardware and warehouse is a little odd.

The sounds of quick footsteps, as if someone were walking in a hurry, are heard on the second floor as well. Not loud thumping footsteps like might be made by a man in heavy work boots, but more of a light, fast step, which makes me think again of the woman seen looking out the window. I've also not heard of the woman being seen looking out the windows of any floor other than the second, which leads me to wonder if she might be limited in her wandering to just that floor for some reason.

Interestingly, I have had one person who saw her looking out the window claim that she responded to him waving at her by waving back. All of the other accounts claim that she doesn't seem to pay attention to anything in particular and doesn't respond at all if someone waves at her; maybe she just liked the look of the young man to whom she waved.

Strangely enough, for a museum filled with historical artifacts, you would think that there would be dozens of paranormal accounts associated with the place, but that doesn't seem to be the case. A lot of the people I spoke to were quick to tell me that there was a lot of activity in the building, but when pressed for details, there just wasn't a lot of information given past the usual type of voices, touching and hair-pulling stories that everyone likes to tell. I wasn't able to come across anyone other than Adrian and Tina Scalf who witnessed anything really cool inside the old building. I couldn't find anyone who had seen an apparition inside the building, saw shadows or strange lights moving about the room or anything else that was unique or especially interesting. What Adrian and Tina saw was a human-shaped shadow that seemed to be watching them all the time from about twelve feet away. It would move when they moved, always keeping a distance between them. They also captured a few good EVPs in the room with the doll exhibit; they were getting intelligent replies to questions asked about the dolls, which was pretty impressive. But for the most part, for a place a cool as the Fort Smith Museum of History, with its working soda fountain and tons of artifacts, there just weren't a lot of interesting ghost stories associated with the place.

GHOSTS OF THE MASSARD PRAIRIE BATTLEFIELD

On the southeast end of Fort Smith, at the junction of Red Pine Drive and Morgan's Way, sits the five-acre park dedicated to an 1864 battle waged between the attacking Confederate forces of about six hundred men and the much smaller Union force of about two hundred men who were defending the outpost. At the time, it was a popular spot to graze horses and livestock, and the outpost was manned by Companies B, D, E and H of the Sixth Kansas Cavalry. The Union troops were camped in a spot that wasn't easily defendable, and the Confederate troops knew it. They attacked at dawn, driving back the pickets and causing the Union troops to form a line basically down the center of their camp. The Confederates attacked from three sides, and it wasn't long before the Federal troops broke and ran, the result being a running battle across two miles of open grassland. In the end, the Confederates captured, wounded or killed close to two companies of the Sixth Kansas, seized much-needed weapons and captured the entire herd of horses. The Battle of Massard Prairie was a firm Southern victory and set the stage for the Battle of Fort Smith, which was to come just a few days later.

Much of the original Massard battlefield has been developed, with neighborhoods leading right up to the park. The remaining bit of it that was preserved, about five acres, contains the parade ground, the mess (kitchen) area and the campsites of Companies B and D. Historical signs mark the location of the areas within the park as well as give a concise description of the battle.

But it would seem that the park and the neighborhoods around it still have a bit of the Civil War raging around them. Reports of the sounds of battle, the shouts and cries of men and the sounds of horses have all been reported. Several of the residents of the neighborhood that leads to the park were reluctant to talk to me about any paranormal activity that they might have seen in the neighborhood or while in the park; it seems that having Civil War ghosts still fighting and running about the place isn't that good for property values. A few of them did speak up about some strange things they've seen around their homes and in the park, and a few of them had pretty good stories. One person told me about the ghost of a Union soldier that kept looking in their back window at night while they were watching TV, which I found to be pretty funny. It happened every night for a few weeks after they moved into the house and didn't stop until the homeowner walked outside and told him in a very loud voice to knock it off, as he was scaring the kids. Although they never saw the spirit look through the window again, the man who owned the home was sitting out in the backyard one evening after work, grilling and having a beer, when he heard a man's voice say hello. He figures that it was the soldier who was curious about them watching TV and who was just trying to be polite. The man said hello back and went on with his grilling. He said neither he nor his family has ever witnessed anything since. Another person from the neighborhood told me an interesting story about the park itself and the soldiers that still seem to inhabit it.

The Running Battle

Steve lives in the neighborhood close to the park and likes to get up early in the morning and walk/run for a while to get his exercise in for the day. Retired for a few years now, he has a bit of time on his hands and likes to get out while the weather is nice and just poke around the park.

One morning, he had been out walking and decided to stop inside the park and take a break. It was early, between 0600 and 0700, and was a really warm July morning but still quite nice out. There was not a cloud in the sky and just a slight breeze. He remembered wondering if it might have been like that the morning of the battle. He was about to find out.

As he sat there taking a break, he heard what sounded like men arguing, but the louder it got, the more he realized it wasn't an argument so much as it was men yelling back and forth to one another. As he sat there listening, he started hearing what sounded like horses whinnying and the clanks and bangs of things being moved and thrown around. Completely curious, he got up and started walking in the direction of the yelling to see what was going on. Now, as he likes to point out, the park isn't really all that big, and it's not what you would consider to be densely wooded. It is a prairie, after all. So he was walking and looking, trying to pinpoint exactly where the noise was coming from. As he walked, he could hear more men shouting, more noise and what he was sure was gunfire—lots of it. He just stopped and stood very still at that point, unsure of what was going on, and as the sounds of gunfire got louder, he crouched down on the ground—an instinctual move to make a smaller target of himself.

As he crouched there, he heard the sounds of men running past him, the yelling, the screams and the sounds of gunfire—everything that you would expect to hear in a battle, minus the actual participants. It seemed to come from all around him as if he was right in the middle of it all. While the whole thing was pretty strange, the part that he had the most trouble wrapping his head around was the sound of someone dying right next to him. About a foot or two from where he was hunkered down, he heard a *thud* as if something hit the ground with a lot of force. He immediately heard a loud cry followed by moaning. A moment later, he heard what he described as a "death rattle"—the sighing, ragged last breath of a man dying. A moment later and it was all gone. No yelling, no sounds of horses, no gunfire—just a quiet, beautiful morning. As he slowly stood up, he looked all around him, half expecting to see the ground littered with bodies, but nothing at all was there—just tall grass moving slightly in the breeze.

Steve is convinced that what he heard that July morning was some ghostly remnant of the battle that played out there in 1864. He simply doesn't see any other rational explanation for it, and from the sound of it, he could be right. I walked down to the park with him, and he showed me exactly where what he witnessed took place. It's an open area for the most part, just as he described it, and one of the things that I thought of was the possibility of sound carrying from the neighborhood. Maybe someone was watching an old war movie with the window open and the TV up loud, and the sound simply carried to where Steve was walking. But after walking down there with him, it became apparent that it would have needed to be one really loud movie for the sound to carry that far, not to mention that it would have drawn a few complaints from the neighbors at that time of the morning. And that wouldn't explain the thud and the death rattle that he claimed to have heard. There are many accounts of people hearing the sounds of battle and, in some cases, even witnessing a ghostly version of the battle play out before them. I certainly can't see any reason why it couldn't have happened that morning at the Massard Prairie Battlefield Park too.

The Union Soldier

Another story that I heard associated with the battlefield park concerns the apparition of a Union soldier. While I was visiting the park, I took the time to walk around with my Mel Meter to see if I could pick up any electromagnetic field fluctuations where there shouldn't have been any. Interestingly enough, a young lady and her husband were there at the same time and saw what I was doing. She was an admitted ghost hunting show addict and recognized my Mel Meter right away. She asked if I was looking for ghosts. I explained to her that I was merely sweeping for any anomalies that I might find and not necessarily hunting ghosts, although if one decided to pop up in front of me I wouldn't be disappointed at all. They told me that the previous summer (2017), they had experienced the apparition of a Union soldier while at the park.

They were walking around the park checking things out, just enjoying the afternoon and the fact that they were about the only people there. It was quiet and pleasant, and they were just walking along holding hands and chatting when a Union soldier appeared right in front of them. He was running like the very devil himself was chasing him, looking over his shoulder as he ran. As they stood there, open-mouthed in disbelief, they heard a shot ring out, and the running soldier pitched forward onto his face in the dirt. Struggling, the soldier rolled over onto his back, and as they watched, he threw his hands up in front of him as if pleading for his life. Another shot rang out, and the soldier's head snapped back, bouncing off the ground. Then he lay still. A moment later, he faded from sight as they stood there in a mild state of shock.

They looked all around them, but there was no one else anywhere close and both shots were very loud and close. Admittedly, they were both scared by what they had just seen, but they were curious as well, so they cautiously walked over to where they had seen the fallen soldier shot to see if there were any marks on the ground or anything to prove that they hadn't just imagined it all. There was nothing to see—no blood, no marks in the dirt, nothing—but the one thing that they both experienced while standing there was a feeling of electricity in the air. The hair on their arms and necks was standing on end, and the temperature in that immediate area seemed noticeably cooler by several degrees or so like they had walked into a pocket of cold air. They said they looked at each other for a minute and then broke out in a dead run for their car. They were laughing about it as they told me the story, but they assured me that it wasn't so funny the day they experienced it.

She said that they come back regularly, hoping that they might see something else, but other than the occasional shout or feeling like they just walked through a huge tangle of spiderwebs, they've never experienced anything paranormal in nature since then.

Battlefields have always held a certain fascination for me. The violence, the loss of life and the emotional stress that was spent on the bloody piece of ground seem to leave a permanent stain on the land. You can't have that number of people in an emotionally charged situation and not have some type of activity remain behind. Every battlefield that I have ever visited has a feel to it, an electricity that seems to run through the air, with more intense pockets of it scattered about. Massard Prairie is no different.

I used my Mel Meter to take random readings around the park, and areas that should have shown nothing but a baseline zero were giving off 2.5 to 6.5 milligauss, with five-degree temperature fluctuations. These weren't "windblown" pockets of EMF, meaning that a possible electrical anomaly was being carried on the wind currents, showing up for a few seconds and then passing on by. They were pockets of steady temperature and EMF fluctuations, holding steady for up to five minutes before dissipating. Is this conclusive evidence that paranormal activity exists at the Massard Prairie Battlefield Park? Not at all, but it is one of those things that makes you wonder if the stories that you hear about the place don't have some merit to them.

Fort Chaffee

A place with an interesting history, Fort Chaffee has long been reputed to be a hot spot of paranormal activity and has even been featured on the paranormal TV show *Ghost Adventures*. First established in 1941 in response to the United States' preparation for what was seen as an almost inevitable outbreak of war, Camp Chaffee was formed from 15,163 acres obtained at a cost of $1.35 million from an assorted 712 property owners.

Named for World War I major general Adna R. Chaffee Jr., an artillery officer who served with distinction, it took about sixteen months to build the entire base, with the first troops arriving on December 7, 1941, the exact day that Pearl Harbor was bombed. From 1942 to 1946, several units trained there, including the Sixth, Fourteenth and Sixteenth Armored Divisions. While the camp served as a training facility during World War II, it also served as a prisoner of war camp, with more than three thousand German POWs being held there.

After the war, Camp Chaffee was home to the Fifth Armored Division from 1948 to 1957, and on March 21, 1956, it was officially upgraded from a camp to a fort, becoming the Fort Chaffee that we know today. In 1958, Elvis Presley entered the army at Fort Chaffee and received his first military haircut in Building 803; the haircut and the media coverage it generated caused some to refer to it as the "haircut heard 'round the world." As a side note, my own personal connection to Elvis Presley, besides researching his presence at Fort Chaffee, was being stationed at Ray Barracks in Friedberg, Germany, the same duty station in the Third Armored Division that he had, although twenty years later. I ate breakfast every morning that we weren't in the field at the Sergeant Elvis Aaron Presley Dining Facility. But I digress once again.

In 1961, Fort Chaffee was declared inactive, although it was later reactivated that same year, and during the Vietnam War, it was used as a test site for Agent Orange and other defoliant chemicals. In keeping with its Vietnam War connection, Fort Chaffee was later used to house Vietnamese refugees from 1975 to 1976. The fort processed more than fifty thousand refugees through its gates, helping them arrange sponsors and gain residence here in the States.

The year 1980 would see the fort pressed into service once more as a refugee center, this time in response to the Cuban Refugee Crisis. A short time after arriving at Fort Chaffee, the refugees rioted and burned two buildings causing state troopers to fire tear gas to break up the riot. It was a rough place at that time and referred to as "the worst duty I ever had" by more than one soldier assigned to guard the fort. Violence was commonplace in the camp, as was prostitution. One soldier who was interviewed claimed that at the time of his interview, there were three whorehouses working, with the going price being one pack of cigarettes—not a fantastic place to be held, for sure. The soldiers assigned to guard the facility and maintain order had a tough job at the very least. In two years, the government processed more than twenty-five thousand Cuban refugees through the gates.

The fort went through several more changes during the years after that, with part of the fort being turned over to the state as surplus land. The remaining sixty-six thousand acres were transferred to the Arkansas National Guard as a training facility in 1997. The fort would see service as a refugee center once more when Hurricane Katrina hit the Gulf Coast in 2005. The empty barracks were converted into temporary housing for more than ten thousand refugees from Louisiana, Mississippi, and Texas.

Today, parts of the fort have burned down, most notably the hospital area, and others have been dismantled; no active-duty troops are assigned there at the time of this writing, and the base serves only in the capacity of a training facility for Reserve and National Guard soldiers.

But while there might not be any active duty troops, POWs or refugees remaining, there was and is a lot of activity still going on at the fort—it's just activity of the paranormal kind.

The Prison Area

Within the Fort Chaffee base enclosure was another enclosure of high fences and barbed wire that saw many uses—first as a holding area for German POWs during World War II, then as a holding area for Vietnamese refugees and finally as a holding area for the Cuban refugees. Within the barbed wire confines of the holding area, the buildings laid out in neat rows, there was another compound within a compound: the solitary confinement area that housed the worst of the worst during the Cuban Refugee Crisis.

During World War II, according to most documents and accounts that I have been able to find, the German POWs were very well behaved, with only a few instances of violence recorded. These consisted mainly of fights and altercations, but nothing resulting in death. As close as I have been able to tell, there were only three deaths at the camp while the Germans were there, and they were all from sickness or natural causes. They did produce an alleged spirit though.

The same held true for the Vietnamese. They were quite well behaved and had a leadership core setup within the camp. There were also entire families and extended families at the camp, and from what I can determine, they were extremely cooperative and quite happy to be here in the States. I found no record of any deaths associated with the time that the Vietnamese were held at Fort Chaffee and hardly any mention at all of violence of any type; they were model citizens, for the most part, it would seem.

That brings us to the Cuban refugees. They were entirely different from the Vietnamese, as they had no family or leadership core in place. At the risk of sounding harsh, they were, as one soldier who guarded the facility said, "The dregs of Cuban society. Castro got rid of all the crazies and criminals by pawning them off on us." Whether his assessment was entirely fair or not is hard to say, but almost from the start, there was violence. A few weeks into their stay, they rioted and burned down a few buildings. The state police responded and broke up the riot with tear gas, and about eighty people were moved into the solitary confinement area.

Homemade knives and other weapons were routinely confiscated, drugs and homemade alcohol were in widespread use and prostitution was going full swing—it was a gritty, violent place. As might be imagined, such a place produced a few deaths. From what I can find, there were several stabbings and one strangulation attributed to the Cubans.

Adrian and Tina Scalf of River Valley Paranormal Research and Investigations have investigated multiple locations within Fort Chaffee, the

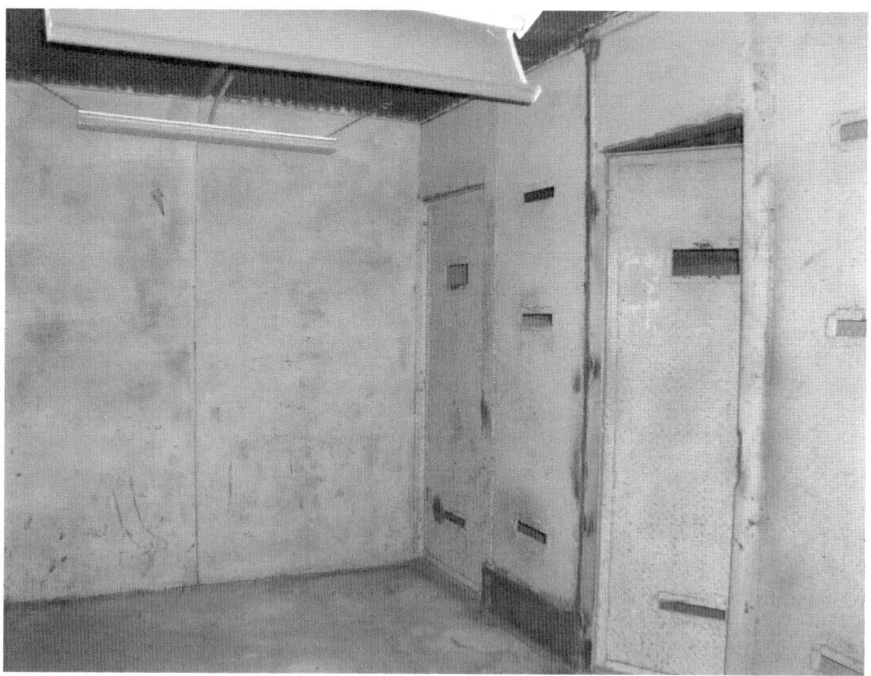

Prison cells inside the old solitary confinement area at Fort Chaffee. *Photo by Adrian Scalf.*

prison being one of them. They told me that they documented several EVPs and saw a lot of shadows moving within the old buildings. There was a different feeling to the air inside the compound as well—a heavy type of feeling, the type that one would almost refer to as oppressive. With all the negative energy that place soaked up, it's little wonder.

I spoke with a former soldier whose last name was Reed several months ago on one of the Facebook military pages. He went on temporary duty assignment several times from Fort Sill Oklahoma to Fort Chaffee for summer training exercises in the mid-1980s and remembered the prison area quite well; he also had an interesting ghost story to tell about it and about the NCO club. He thought the prison area was probably the creepiest place he had ever poked around at in his entire life. We messaged back and forth for about an hour, swapping both military and ghost stories, and the ones he told me about Chaffee were interesting, to say the least.

Reed was on temporary training duty for about two months the first time he went to Fort Chaffee, and at nights after chow (dinner), they were given free rein to do whatever they wanted. A group of them decided to go explore the old buildings around the fort, as quite a few of them were unoccupied at the time—the prison area containing the most of them. He said that the main walkthrough gate to the prison area was open, so they just walked right on in, pausing for a moment to check out the old guard shack and then moving on to the barracks buildings. They went in a few of the old buildings, but there wasn't much to see—just large open bay rooms with bathrooms at the end. Some of the walls had graffiti written on them and a few words in Spanish were carved on the bathroom doors, but other than a broken window or two, they were just pretty ordinary buildings.

He thought that it was around the fourth building they investigated that things started to go a little sideways. He said that you could almost feel a heavy static electric charge in the air from the moment you stepped foot inside. They all felt it, but no one wanted to admit that they were creeped out by it, so they went on inside and had a closer look around. They walked into the open bay and stopped in the center of the room, looking all around but not really seeing anything of interest. Just as they were getting ready to leave, they saw a dark shadow figure dart across the room and disappear into the bathroom. Reed admitted that it both startled and scared them a little bit, but being young and soldiers to boot, there was no way in hell they would have admitted that fact to one another; it was decided that they would ease on across the room and have a look inside the bathroom.

Reed said he was pushed to the front of the group as they got near the bathroom area, and he leaned in to get a better look at the inside before committing himself to walk in. He said he should have seen it coming, but a good hard shove from one of his friends placed him several feet inside the bathroom before he even realized what had happened. As he spun around to chew them out, the bathroom door suddenly slammed shut in their faces, leaving him all alone in the bathroom. He jumped over to the door to wrench it back open, but it seemed to be stuck. For a moment, he thought maybe his friends were holding it shut from the other side. He abandoned that thought when he heard them hollering for him and pounding on the door a few seconds later. He shouted back that the door was stuck, and one of his friends told him to stand back—they were going to kick it in. He could hear them kicking time and again, but the door never budged.

Reed said he was more than a little freaked out and turned around to survey the bathroom in front of him; that's when he saw the shadow figure again. It stepped out of a stall and just stood there looking at him, or at least he guessed it was looking at him, as it didn't have a face or anything other than a human form that was completely black. He said it cocked its head

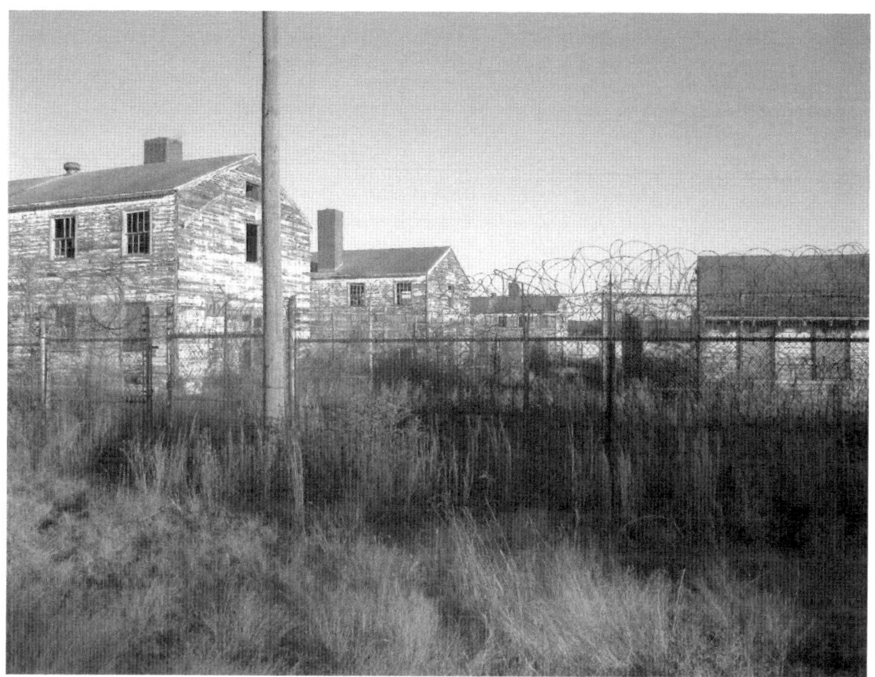

The prison area at Fort Chaffee. It's said to host a lot of paranormal activity, including several shadow figures. *Photo by Adrian Scalf.*

from side to side a few times and took a few steps toward him before stopping again. Reed told me that he was frozen in place, so scared he didn't even think to yell for his friends. He said it kept cocking its head from side to side, and then suddenly it darted toward the wall, stopped, turned around and darted back into a stall. All of the stall doors started opening and shutting with so much force that the entire connecting walls of the toilet section were shaking and shuddering. Reed said he found his voice then and started screaming for his friends to help him and banging on the door.

A second later, he grabbed the door handle and pulled on the door as hard as he could; it swung open easily as if it had never been stuck, and Reed cut out for the outside door as fast as his feet would carry him, his buddies following close on his heels. They didn't stop until they were well outside the compound and away from the buildings. It was then that Reed told his friends what he had seen in the bathroom. To his surprise, they had seen something similar darting from wall to wall in the open bay at the same time that he was trying to get out of the bathroom. According to his friends, when the bathroom door slammed shut and refused to open, one of them had turned away from the door for a moment to look around for something that they might use to pry open the door. It was then that he saw the shadow figure dart from one wall to the other and pause there for a moment before darting back to the other side. He hollered for his friends, and they all turned around and saw it as well; it just kept going back and forth across the room, getting a little closer to them each time. It was within twenty feet of them when the door opened and Reed made a dash for the outside.

After comparing stories for a few moments, they took off at a brisk trot toward the NCO club and spent the rest of the evening having a few beers and trying to wrap their heads around what they had all just experienced. Reed said that before the experience, he had been a huge skeptic about the supernatural and thought that it was all just stories made up to try and scare simple-minded people. After what happened, he had a huge change of heart and now readily admits that he is sure that there are more things in the world unseen and unknown than we will ever be able to understand.

Reed says that he can laugh about the experience now, but when it happened and for a time afterward, he was uncomfortable being alone. He also says that it made him more aware of the world around him, and he started noticing other unusual things. His second trip back to Fort Chaffee netted another experience for him, although not as scary for him as the prison experience, and this time it happened in a nearly empty NCO club.

The NCO Club

Reed had accompanied a group of his friends to the NCO club for a few beers and some pizza after a full day of training. It had been a long day, and as the evening wore on, pretty soon some of the members of his party started to call it a night and head back to the barracks until it was just Reed and another soldier named Giles. The only other person in the club was the bartender, who was lounging at the end of the bar, nose stuck in a book. Reed and Giles were at one end of the club at a table, and the bartender was at the other end of the room, with about thirty feet separating them. All of a sudden, an empty beer bottle that had been left on the bar top flew across the room and broke against the wall. Reed said that everyone stopped talking and looked all around to see what had happened, and the bartender asked if they had thrown the bottle. Both men denied doing it, and about that time, they watched another beer bottle slowly slide all the way down the bar top and come to a stop a foot or so away from the bartender. It paused there for a moment and then slowly slid back down the bar and stopped again.

As the men watched in amazement, the bottle raised up in the air and flew across the room to shatter in the same spot as the first bottle. Reed and Giles both jumped to their feet, looking all around, and the bartender set his book aside and was standing there with his mouth open, just looking at the broken glass on the floor. As all three of the men stood there, unsure of what had just happened, they all heard a clearly audible laugh that seemed to come from everywhere at once, as if it was all around them. That was enough for Reed and Giles, and without much hesitation, they said goodnight to the bartender and got ready to leave. Reed said he remembered the bartender asking them to stick around for a little bit and offered to buy them a few beers if they would stay. The guy obviously didn't want to stay there by himself. Both men declined his offer without hesitation.

Reed told me that he has experienced other things over the years since then, but nothing like what he witnessed both times while at Fort Chaffee. I asked him if he has ever thought about going back and checking the old fort out again just to see if anything else might happen; his answer was pretty short: just a "no" and that was it. I guess he's not in any hurry to see if whatever was there might remember him or not.

The Medical Complex

One of the best-known haunted areas on Fort Chaffee and one that was featured on the *Ghost Adventures* TV show was the hospital area or medical complex. Unfortunately, it burned to the ground in August 2011 in a fire that consumed more than one hundred buildings and eighty acres of ground. It was a terrible loss both from the historical aspect and the paranormal. Built in two parts over 1941 and 1942, the complex had an 834-bed hospital, three mess halls, a post exchange, a post office, and barracks. It also had an emergency room, an operating room, and a few solitary confinement cells. The medical facility was like a complex within a complex.

Adrian and Tina Scalf of River Valley Paranormal Research and Investigations were fortunate enough to investigate the medical complex on several occasions, once with the *Ghost Adventures* team. They remembered the sounds of heavy footsteps behind them while they were in the complex—footsteps so loud that they thought someone was behind them—and turned

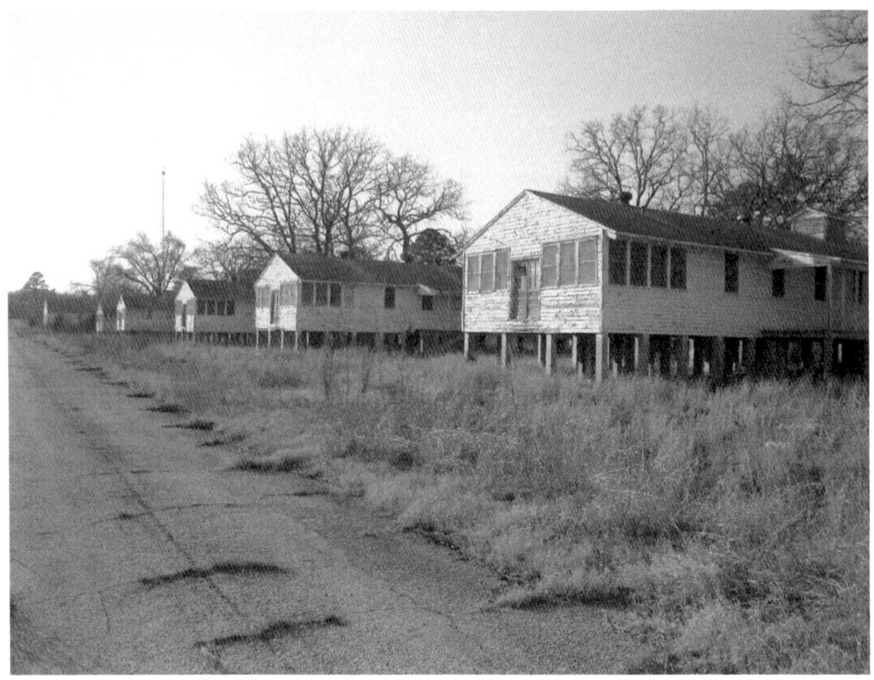

The overgrown medical complex before it burned. It was a huge maze of buildings that were highly active. *Photo by Adrian Scalf.*

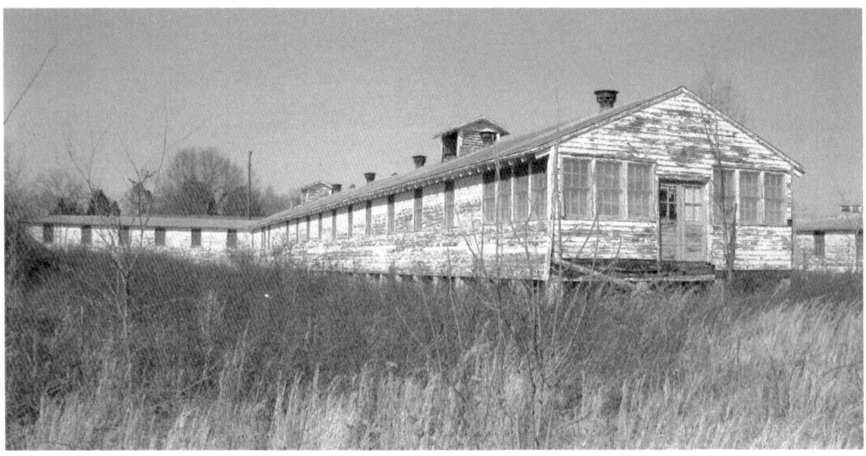

Another view of one of the medical complex buildings before the complex burned to the ground. *Photo by Adrian Scalf.*

around to shine the flashlight on whoever might be there, but there was never anyone there. They also documented several EVPs while in the complex, some of which said, "Help" and "We need help," along with one that asked, "What do you want?" They said that it was always an active location and was investigated by quite a few different paranormal investigation and research teams over the years; it was a sad day when it burned down.

Some of the reported activity included EVPs, shadow figures that seemed to roam the hallways and clearly audible voices that were sometimes engaged in conversation or seemed to be crying out; on several occasions, the full-bodied apparition of a man in uniform was seen. While there are numerous stories of experiences and documented evidence, strangely enough, there aren't that many stories connected with the medical complex outside of the usual paranormal activity—no shocking stories like those associated with the prison area. For a complex that was investigated so many times and was even featured on a TV show, I thought that there would have been a truckload of awesome stories associated with it, but I just wasn't able to find any that were too remarkable.

While I have never had the pleasure of investigating Fort Chaffee, it is a place that has been on my bucket list for quite some time. Having been in the army, attached to an armored division, and having spent a lot of time in the old open bay barracks that were all over Fort Chaffee, I have a familiarity with old military bases. I understand the people who were stationed there, the jobs they did and the sometimes off-color fun that young soldiers engaged in; I can relate to the place. Even though a lot of the old buildings have burned down, including the medical complex, there are still a lot of active locations scattered around the fort, and I can't help but wonder that even though the buildings might be gone, the spirits might still remain in some fashion or other. It would certainly be interesting to find out.

PART II

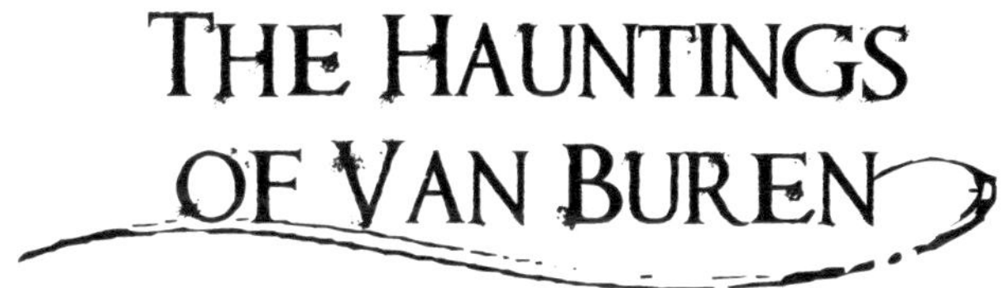

The Hauntings of Van Buren

Like Fort Smith across the river, Van Buren has a lot of interesting ghost stories associated with it. From the spirit of a young man killed in front of the King Opera House to the ghostly soldier on duty at the Confederate section of the Fairview Cemetery, the stories of the paranormal are out there if a person would take the time to seek them out. And like the stories of the paranormal, the town itself has an interesting history, as well as some intriguing stories to go with it.

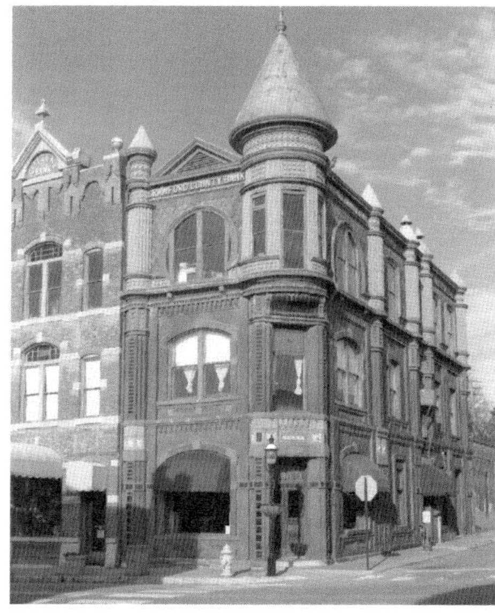

This interesting building was once the old Crawford County Bank. *Photo by Bud Steed.*

The King Opera House

Built in the late nineteenth century, the King Opera House sits at 427 Main Street surrounded by six blocks of restored buildings from the late nineteenth and early twentieth centuries, making up the Main Street National Historic District. These buildings are home to restaurants, shops, and offices, but a visitor can still imagine how it looked back in the early days when some of the buildings were banks, lawyers' offices, and stores. The entire downtown district from the train station to the courthouse is well maintained and quite charming. It's a wonderful place to stop, take a walk and do a little shopping. It's also a great place to spot a ghost or two, according to some of the stories circulating around, and the King Opera House seems to be one of the main spots to have a ghostly encounter.

The Actor

I came across two accounts that seem to suggest the origin of one of the spirits that haunt the opera house. They are both similar in nature but end with a different style of death for the young actor who is the primary character in the story. In the first version, the young man arrives in town as part of a troupe of actors playing an engagement at the King Opera House. Said to be a handsome young man, quite dashing and well thought of among his fellow actors, he almost immediately fell head over heels in

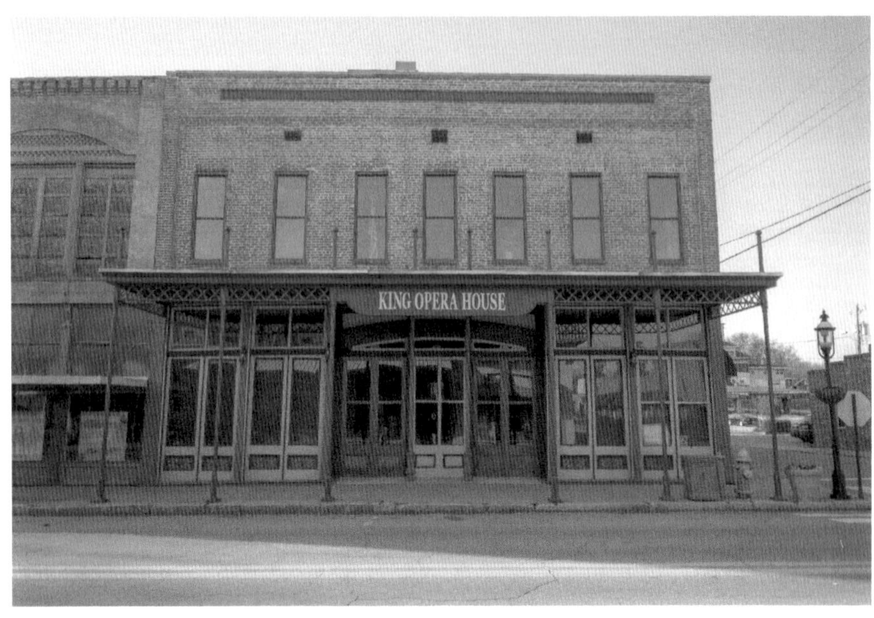

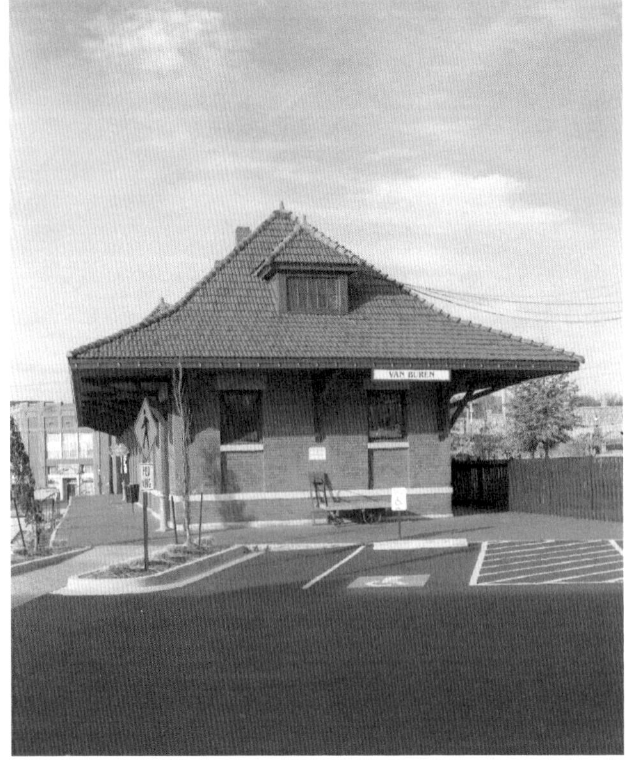

Above: The historic King Opera House. It's said to be haunted by the ghost of an actor who was killed by a disapproving father. *Photo by Adrian Scalf.*

Left: The restored Van Buren train station. *Photo by Bud Steed.*

love with the daughter of the town's prominent doctor. Needless to say, the doctor wasn't all that thrilled with his daughter seeing the young actor, and he forbade them from seeing each other. That set the stage for them to run off together, and plans were made for the young woman to meet the actor at the train station, where they would elope and live happily ever after. Things didn't quite work out that way.

The doctor caught wind of the elopement and drove his buggy to the train station to retrieve his wayward daughter. An argument started between the doctor and the young actor that resulted in the doctor beating the young man severely with a horsewhip. The young man died a short time later from the beating, and his spirit is said to linger around the opera house, the type of place that he certainly would have loved given his occupation.

In the second version of the story, the young actor meets the daughter of a wealthy businessman and falls deeply in love with her. The father denies them their love and forbids them from seeing each other. They secretly meet and decide to run away together, arranging to meet in front of the opera house and then make their way together to the train station to make their escape from her overbearing father. Dear old dad catches wind of the elopement and grabs a pistol, storming down to the opera house, where he finds the young actor impatiently awaiting the arrival of the girl he loves. The angry father confronts the actor, and an argument starts between the two men; it finishes with the father shooting the young actor to death on the sidewalk in front of the opera house. As he lay there dying, the girl he loved rushed to his side; the young man professed his love for her with his last breath.

And so we have the two versions of the possible origin of the alleged ghost that seems to be haunting the King Opera House. Which version is the correct one we will never really know, and as it goes with stories like these, I'm sure there are probably a few more variations that I haven't run across yet. But regardless of which one might be correct, there have been numerous reports of paranormal activity in and around the opera house for many years, and most sightings of an apparition seem to be that of a young man dressed rather nicely in what has been described as a well-fitting suit with a long coat—almost like a tuxedo from the description of it. Most of the activity is attributed to him, and he is thought to be the spirit of the young actor, although this has never been established as fact.

A former employee of the King Opera House whom I spoke with while researching this book told me of an encounter with the young man one night as she was helping secure the building at closing time. Kay had been going around making sure that the lights were off in all the rooms and had started back down the hallway when the lights started flickering on and off. She looked through an open door to her right and saw the outline of a person standing in the room. Thinking that it might be a coworker, she asked what they were doing but got no response. She walked to the door and flipped on the light, but no one was there. Thinking that she had imagined it, she turned off the light in the room and turned to go. As she pulled the door closed behind her, she looked back in the room again and saw the outline of a person standing there again. She immediately flipped on the light, and to her amazement, standing there in the middle of the room was a young man. She described him as being quite good looking, with blond wavy hair and a warm smile.

Kay asked him who he was and what he was doing there? She said the young man got a really sad, almost puzzled look on his face and said, "I'm not really sure anymore." With that, he turned slightly away from her and just disappeared. Kay said she just stood there for a second in shock and then let out a scream and fled down the hallway to the office, where she promptly retold her story to her coworkers who were helping close up. Not really sure what to make of it, they all went together back down the hall to the room and peered inside. No one was there, and there didn't seem to be anything out of the ordinary in the room, so they simply turned off the lights, closed the door and finished closing up the building. Kay told me that now she feels bad about screaming and running away, as the young man didn't seem threatening at all—just a little lost and confused. But at the time it shocked her to simply watch him vanish right in front of her eyes. She said she wonders from time to time if he might still be there, wandering around the building, not really sure who he is or why he is there—a rather sad way to spend the afterlife, in my opinion.

One person had an experience outside the building on the sidewalk as well. They were out for a stroll one night and were passing in front of the King Opera House when a young man in an old Victorian-era suit, complete with top hat, walked around the corner in front of them. Thinking that he was an actor in costume or something, they said hello and complimented the young man on his suit. The young man tipped his hat and smiled at them but never said a word. The person stopped and turned to watch the young man pass by but discovered that no one was there at all. They stated that there was nowhere for the young man to go, nowhere to hide; it was as if he simply disappeared after passing them by.

Whoever the young man might be, whether an actor or just a former patron who likes to hang around the place, he seems to be pretty active. But after a little more digging, I found a report of another spirit that was

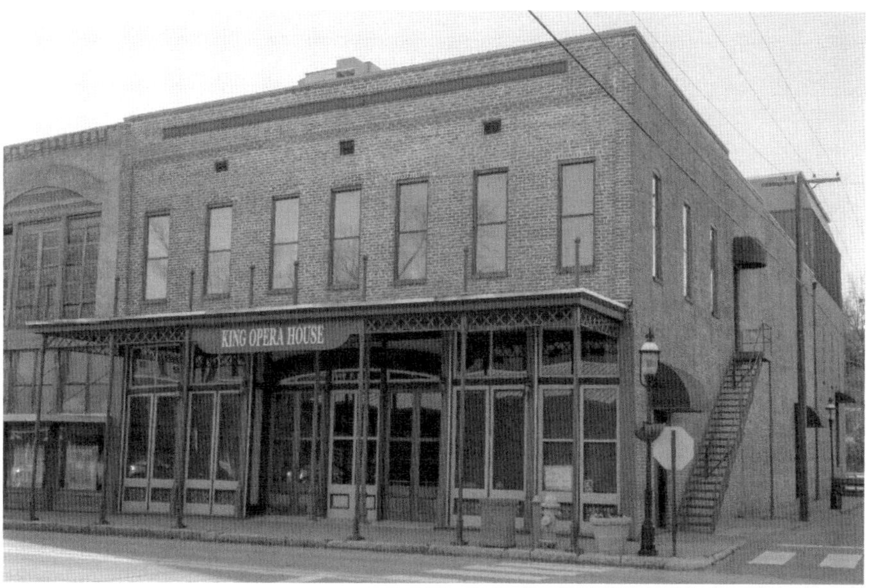

The King Opera House building. *Photo by Adrian Scalf.*

allegedly seen in the opera house, this time a young woman, so perhaps some of the activity attributed to the young man might not all be his doing after all.

The Beautiful Young Woman in White

The spirit connected with this story is said to be that of a beautiful young woman dressed in a flowing white dress, her long dark hair piled up on top of her head and held in place by a large silver clasp of some sort. The person who told me this story was a patron of the opera house and had his experience in the bathroom of all places.

He was standing at the sink washing his hands and said that when he looked up, he saw the reflection of a beautiful young woman that appeared to be standing right behind him. He was amused that she was there and turned around to tell her that she was in the wrong bathroom. He described her as slender, having dark hair and blue eyes, and she was wearing an old-fashioned high-necked white dress that flowed all the way down to the floor. He said she just stood there looking at him for a moment and then asked him, "Have you seen Henry by chance? I can't seem to find him anywhere." The man told her that he didn't know anyone named Henry but that he would be happy to walk with her to the office and see if they might be able to help. He said she just smiled at him, shook her head no and then turned to walk away. She took several steps toward the door and then just faded from sight. He just stood there for a moment or two and then left the bathroom to find his wife and tell her what had just happened. She asked him if the young woman might be a patron as well and had simply walked out the door, but the man was adamant that she had disappeared into thin air. He said she was several feet from the door when she vanished.

Who the beautiful young woman is and why she is hanging out at the opera house, most specifically in the men's room at the opera house, is anyone's guess. The gentleman's story is the only one that I have run across concerning the woman; most of them concern the young man that seems to haunt the location. One can't help but wonder if she might be the young girl that the actor was so in love with, searching for him in vain, or perhaps they are both haunting the building together and she just lost track of him for a moment. No one really knows for sure or even if either story has any factual basis to them, but if they are true and she is the girl the young actor was crazy about, I'd like to think that they found each other and are together for eternity. I'm a sucker for a happy ending.

Other reports of activity inside the building are frequent—everything from lights turning on and off by themselves to water faucets turning on, doors opening on their own, the sound of voices, being touched, clothing tugged on and the feeling of being watched and not being alone in a room even though no one else is there. Why a building such as the King Opera House would have so much alleged activity is the million-dollar question. Does it stem from lost love and violent death, or does it go toward the other end of the spectrum and revolve around the joy and happiness that the place brought to so many people? While the stories of the ghosts and hauntings can't be confirmed, the fact that so many people enjoyed themselves at the opera house is just a given—it was a source of entertainment, employment, and happiness for a large number of people. I would like to think that the King Opera House is haunted not just because of one alleged death but because it meant a lot to a great number of people and because maybe they had such a good time there that a few of them just don't want to leave. That's what I would like to think.

Fairview Cemetery

Established on ten acres of ground donated by John Drennen in 1846 as a community burial ground, the first burial here actually dates back to 1816. Many of the area's first citizens are buried there, including John Drennen himself. The cemetery also holds a large number of Confederate soldiers at a plot of ground donated in the cemetery by the City of Van Buren around 1861. It's estimated that about one hundred Confederate soldiers died while stationed in Van Buren, most from some type of illness, with the remaining soldiers being moved there from various battlefield burial sites after the war had come to a close; about four hundred of those are marked "Unknown."

The cemetery also holds the remains of black Union soldiers who, interestingly enough, were not buried at the Fort Smith National Cemetery among the other U.S. Colored Troops. In 2005, a project to identify and memorialize those African American troops who fought for their freedom resulted in the placing of eight marble military markers inscribed with their names and unit. For an interesting read on these soldiers as well as the African American history of Crawford County, check out the website at arkansasfreedmen.com.

Situated on the high ground overlooking both Van Buren and the river, the Union artillery set up gun emplacements and engaged the Confederate artillery across the river during the Battle of Van Buren. The town received a lot of damage during the shelling, with civilians being among the casualties. The Union guns outnumbered the Confederate artillery; additionally,

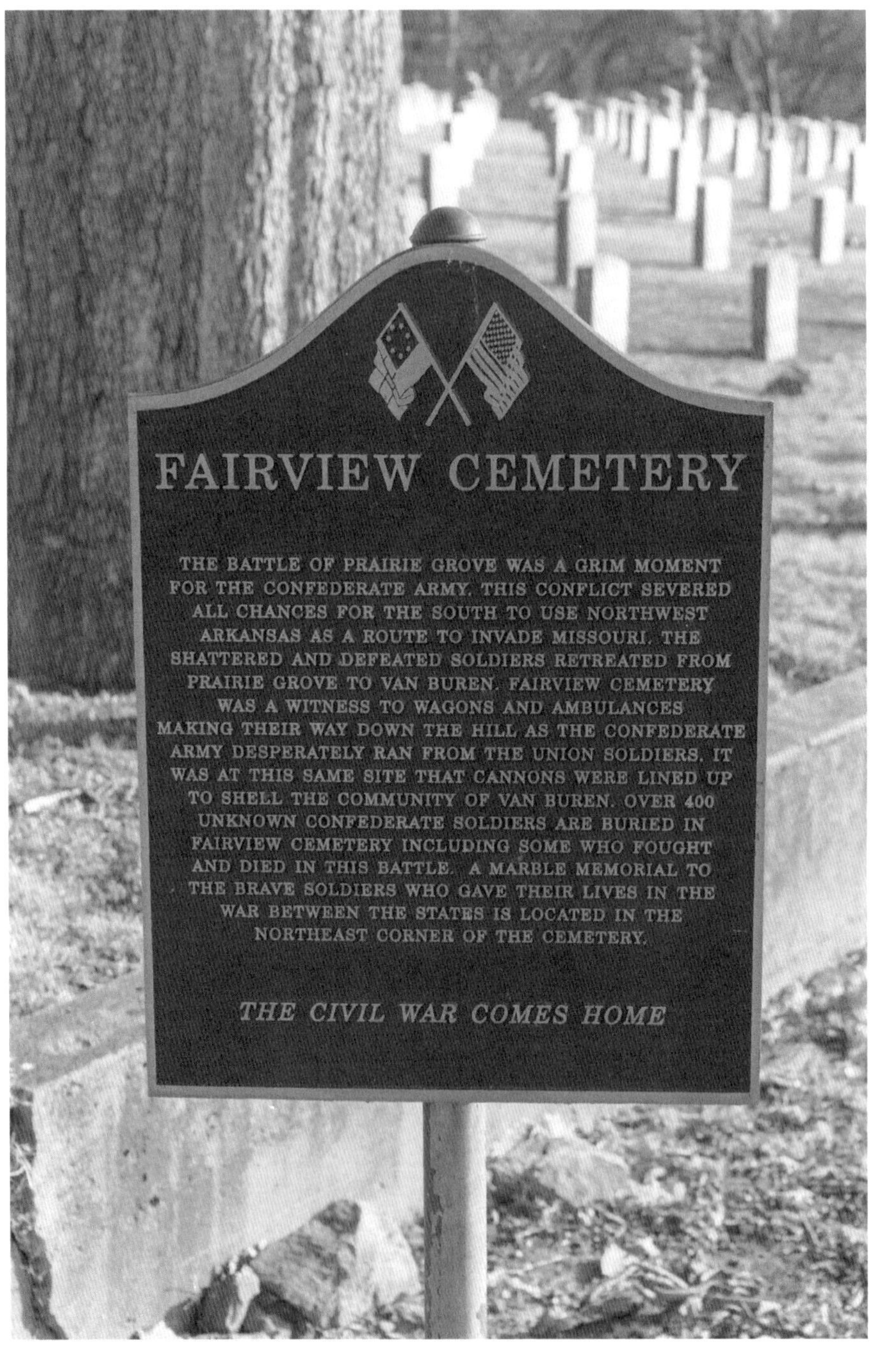

Historical sign about Fairview Cemetery. *Photo by Bud Steed.*

by holding the high ground, they had increased range, soon forcing the Confederates to abandon shelling the town.

In 1873, a Ladies' Southern Memorial Association chapter was formed to help care for the graves of the Confederate dead, but about twenty-three years later, that duty was assumed by the Mary Lee chapter of the United Daughters of the Confederacy (UDC). Several years later, the members erected a memorial in the Confederate section of the cemetery; the monument would later be moved to a more visible location at the Crawford County Courthouse around 1906. A granite marker was later placed at the site of the original monument and is still there today. The Confederate section of the cemetery was placed in the National Register of Historic Places in 1996, with the entire cemetery being placed in the register in 2005; it's a very well-cared-for historic cemetery.

The cemetery sits on Highway 59 just north of downtown Van Buren and is surrounded by neighborhoods on all sides; it is open to the public from sunrise to sunset.

The Confederate Soldier

This particular type of ghost sighting is so common that I almost hesitated to include it in the book, considering I had included one account from the Fort Smith National Cemetery already. It seems as if every military cemetery—Confederate, Union or otherwise—has a ghostly soldier standing guard over his fallen comrades. But as common as it might be, the stories told in connection with the Fairview Cemetery deserve to be told anyway.

This story was told to me by a rather feisty elderly gentleman who frequently walks his dog past the cemetery. I had stopped and was taking some of the photos of the cemetery for this book when the gentleman stopped me and asked me what I was doing. I explained to him that I was a writer and I was writing a book about ghosts and hauntings associated with the area, had heard several stories about the cemetery and wanted to get photos of it to go along with the book. He said that he thought it was an unusual topic to write a book about, and then he asked me if I would like to hear a ghost story about the cemetery that he had personally witnessed. I told him that I most definitely would love to hear his story, so I walked on down the sidewalk with him while he pointed out where it happened and told me what he had seen.

A few years earlier, he had been out taking a walk with his dog, just enjoying the night air. He said it was a clear, warm summer night with a half moon, and the stars were so bright in the sky that they looked like "little flashlights" gleaming in the darkness. I remarked that I had never heard anyone refer to the stars as little flashlights before. Well, the old man stopped, turned to look at me and said, "Are you going to keep interrupting me, or do you want to hear the story?" I apologized and asked him to please continue.

As he was walking, he thought he could see someone moving about in the Confederate section of the cemetery. They would be there one instant and then gone from sight the next, so his first thought was that it was someone who was up to no good; why else would anyone be in a cemetery at night, stooping over and disappearing every few moments? He decided to investigate, as he thought that they might be vandals desecrating the graveyard, and he wasn't about to let anyone get away with that without at least confronting them. So, just as bold as you please, he marched up the lane into the cemetery, right up to the Confederate section and said, "You there! What are you doing? No one's supposed to be here after dark." As he stood there peering toward the headstones, a man stepped out from behind a tree a little ways away and just stood there, halfway hidden in the shadows.

"I asked you what you are doing here?" He didn't get a response at all. The man just stood there by the tree for a few moments and then stepped out of the shadows. The elderly gentleman said you could have knocked him over with a feather he was so shocked. There in front of him, clearly visible in the moonlight, was a man dressed in a Civil War uniform, hat and all. The ghost raised his hand as if in recognition of what the man had said and then pointed toward the gravestones. Without a word, he walked over to one of the stones and pointed down at it.

The elderly gentleman who was telling me the story stopped for a moment on the sidewalk and looked at me. "I wasn't the least bit scared! I was a soldier myself. Fought in Korea too, by God," is what he told me as he glanced out into the cemetery for a moment and then continued on with the story.

The soldier motioned for the elderly man to come forward, and to his credit, at least to hear him tell it anyway, he marched right on up to where the ghostly soldier was pointing at the headstone. He looked at the headstone in the moonlight and could clearly see it said "Unknown" on it. The ghost soldier looked at the man and said, "That there's why I'm here." The old man asked him if he was buried there, to which the soldier nodded his head. He also asked him his name but got no reply; the ghost soldier just stood there looking back and forth from the grave marker to the elderly man. The

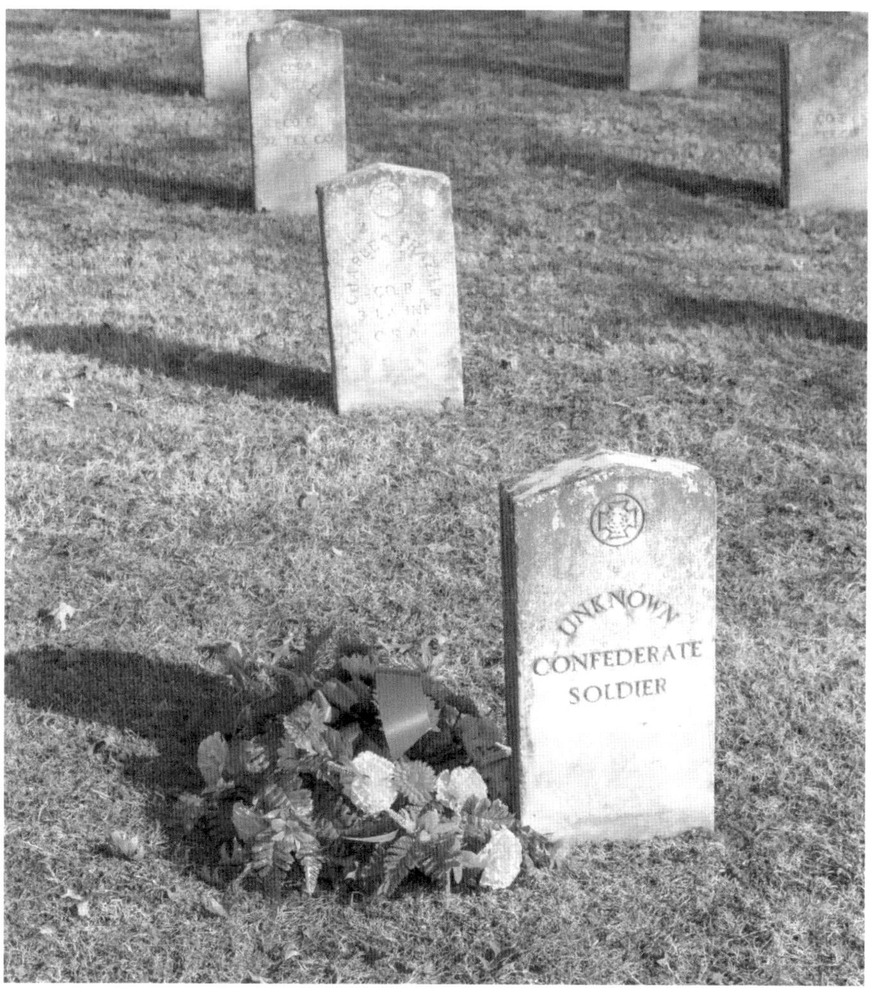

Flowers decorating the grave of an unknown Confederate soldier at Fairview Cemetery. *Photo by Bud Steed.*

man said he asked the soldier why he stuck around such a place all these years, to which he got no reply; the soldier simply waved his arm in the direction of all the other grave markers and then faded from sight as the old man just stood there watching.

He told me he just stood there for a few minutes thinking about what had happened. He wasn't scared, never felt threatened and didn't even feel ill at ease; the whole incident felt as if he was just having a few words with an ordinary stranger. Shoot, even his dog never barked or acted up the entire time it happened; he had just stood there with his tail wagging back and forth. He remembered saying out loud as he turned to leave, "You might be unknown, but you aren't forgotten, soldier. Godspeed and rest well." With that, he walked on out of the cemetery and continued along with his walk, the dog following along right beside him.

He said he thought a lot about the soldier over the next few weeks, but he kept what happened to himself. He thought people would think he was crazy if he told anyone and said that those "money-grubbing kids of mine are just looking for an excuse to lock me up in an old folks home." After a bit, he started putting plastic flowers on the soldier's grave; real ones didn't last long enough, and it was getting harder for him to get out and get to the stores. He didn't figure the ghost soldier would care in the least bit if they were real or not. He told me that he stands there from time to time and talks to the grave too, sharing stories from when he was in Korea. He said he doesn't know for sure if the soldier can hear him or not, but sometimes it's just good to talk out the old stuff anyway. He stopped again on the sidewalk and gave me a really long, almost defiant, look.

"You think I'm crazy? Not altogether there to ramble on about ghosts and such?" I assured him that I didn't think he was crazy in the least bit and thanked him for sharing his story with me; I also shook his hand and thanked him for his service. He was definitely a feisty old guy, and I was fortunate to get to meet him. I think that running across him was the best part of researching this book.

The Little Girl

Another story that I have heard associated with the Fairview Cemetery, and several other cemeteries around the country, is that of the little girl who is seen playing from time to time among the headstones. Described as being about eight or nine years old, with long curly hair and dressed in a long Victorian-style dress, she runs back and forth among the tombstones, crouching down from time to time as if playing hide-and-seek with someone. No noise or sounds are ever heard; she is completely silent, both in voice and in movement. Usually seen in the area between the Confederate section and the private plots that have a short iron fence around them, she simply seems to be having a good old time playing by herself or with an unseen playmate.

Several people have tried approaching her, thinking that she was a real live little girl. They thought that perhaps she was lost, and at the very least, they had to have wondered why a little girl would be playing in a cemetery. Whenever they would call out to her or try and approach, she would disappear before they ever got close, leaving the witness standing there scratching their head in bewilderment.

Apparently, she doesn't seem to interact with anyone, but to me, if the accounts are true, she doesn't seem to be a residual haunting, as she is intelligent enough to disappear when approached or called out to. A residual haunting wouldn't acknowledge a living person's presence let alone vanish because of it. But whether it is a true story or just an urban legend, it needs to be taken with a grain of salt. Sightings like this could easily be explained away as just a neighborhood kid playing in the graveyard who disappears from sight because everyone has told them to stay away from strangers. Like the so-called paranormal phenomenon of "orbs," there are just too many logical ways to explain this one as not being paranormal, but that's just my take on it. Yours might be totally different.

The Dancing Lights

An unusual story associated with the cemetery is that of the "dancing lights." Now, stories of people seeing so-called cemetery lights aren't all that unusual; they're seen all the time in one cemetery or another. They are most often attributed to "swamp gas," lights reflecting off some type of flying bug or bat or myriad other rational explanations, and most people don't place much faith in them being supernatural in any fashion at all. However, sometimes you run across that story that makes you scratch your head and wonder. This is one of those stories.

I've heard this story on at least three separate occasions where the Fairview Cemetery is concerned, one time from a group of four people who watched it from a front porch across the street from the cemetery entrance. It was about 11:00 p.m. on a Saturday night and two couples were just sitting on the porch, having a drink and enjoying the flow of conversation. They were having a good time, laughing and joking, when all of a sudden one of the men stopped in mid-sentence and just sat there staring out at the cemetery. Then the rest of them saw them too: four bright lights, about the size of a softball, were darting around the cemetery at an unusually high rate of speed.

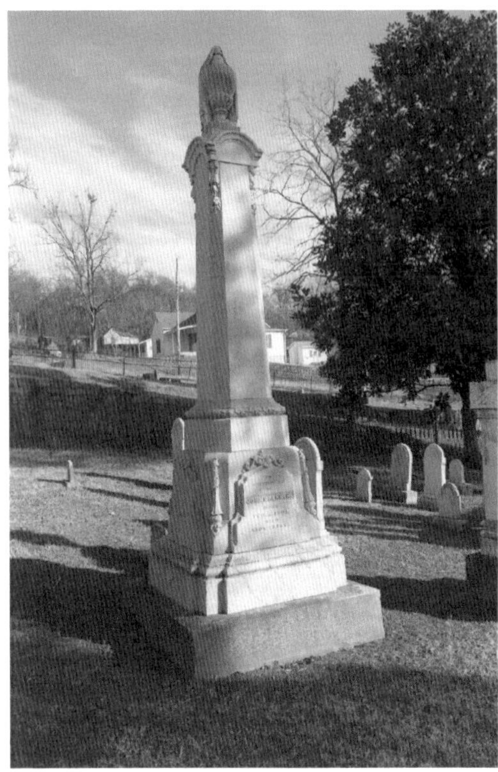

Headstone of John Drennen, one of the founders of Van Buren. *Photo by Bud Steed.*

They all started asking, "Did y'all just see that?" while sitting up a bit straighter in their chairs. As they watched the lights, they thought that perhaps someone, or several someones, was playing a joke on them with flashlights, but there didn't seem to be anyone around. The lights would bob back and forth among the tombstones and then go up really high for a few seconds before plummeting back down to start all over again with the darting back and forth. And while that might not be considered so unusual in some people's book, what happened next was.

The lights suddenly stopped darting around, moved in close to one another and began what one of the ladies referred to as a slow dance. The lights split into two groups and slowly started spinning around one another, weaving and moving from side to side and front to rear as if moving to some unheard music; they were in perfect synchronization, each pair moving exactly the same as the other. This went on for a good five minutes, with the couples mesmerized by the spinning lights. Suddenly, the lights stopped and just hovered there about four feet off the ground. The lights in each pair merged into one, and then the remaining two lights merged together to form one very large bright light. It just hung there in the air for a few minutes before slowly sinking down out of sight behind a tombstone.

The couples on the porch were both excited and completely wigged out at the same time. One of the men rushed inside and grabbed a flashlight, and all four of them took off across the street and into the cemetery to see if they could locate the lights or find some logical solution for what they had just seen. No matter how hard they searched, they couldn't come up with a rational reason for what they had witnessed. They made it a point to keep an eye on the cemetery each night for the next few weeks, hoping to catch a glimpse of the dancing lights again, but they haven't seen them since.

Fairview Cemetery has a rich historical background behind it and numerous connections to the founding of the area and the city of Van Buren. And like most cemeteries that are old, it has some stories of paranormal activity associated with it; the two just seem to go hand in hand, it seems. Whether the stories are true or not is anyone's guess, but I do find it interesting that Fairview, like so many other cemeteries across the country, seems to have at least one story that is similar to, if not the same, as some of the others. The question that arises is this: Why do most of the cemetery stories so closely resemble one another? Some people might point to the Internet and say that it is the cause of certain stories being adopted into the culture of one area from another. While this might be the case in some instances, I was collecting stories and researching alleged paranormal phenomena long before the Internet became part of our society, and I remember hearing a lot of the same stories in a multitude of different areas. While I doubt anyone will ever come up with a concrete answer to this, the fact remains that if you talk to the people who have witnessed it, regardless of the area, they are all pretty adamant about what they witnessed. The same is true of the stories associated with the Fairview Cemetery—those who saw it, those who witnessed it firsthand, are all of the same minds and have the same conclusion: whatever it was, it was very real.

Super 8 Motel

Located on Highway 59 close to Interstate 40, the Super 8 Motel looks like any other motel close to a highway. If you were to stand out the parking lot and take a look at it, it wouldn't seem to be special at all—just an average peaceful roadside motel. But it seems that in a few of the rooms, things aren't quite as peaceful as they appear. The land the motel and the other surrounding businesses are built on saw some conflict and bloodshed during the Battle of Van Buren, as well as in some other smaller skirmishes during the Civil War. That's where the ghost of the Civil War soldier that's seen from time to time most likely originated from.

The Soldier in the Motel Room

I met Carol, her husband and their two children at the Waffle House on Highway 59, just down from the Super 8 Motel. I like to eat at Waffle House. Not what one would consider a sophisticated restaurant, but then I'm not a sophisticated guy. I like good food and plenty of it, and as a few of my ex-wives would happily point out, I'm kind of cheap and I'm okay with that.

I was wearing my TOPS (The Ozarks Paranormal Society) T-shirt that morning and was sitting in the booth savoring my first cup of coffee for the day when I heard a lady's voice behind me say, "Excuse me, sir? Are you one of those ghost hunter guys?" Now, between me and you, I cringe inside when someone calls me a "ghost hunter." I don't creep around in the dark with a ghost gun and a ghost permit looking to bag a ghostly wall hanger kind of trophy—it's not what I do. I investigate and research alleged claims of paranormal activity and document whatever evidence that I am fortunate enough to collect. So, with that in mind, I turned around in the booth and, dying just a little bit inside, said, "Yes, ma'am, I certainly am." She apologized for bothering me and asked if she could ask me a few questions. I told her I would be happy to answer anything that I was able to and asked her what seemed to be troubling her.

After introductions were made all around, she proceeded to tell me about an experience that they had the night before at the Super 8 Motel. Carol and her family are from a little town outside Jackson, Tennessee, and were just starting out on the first leg of a grand family vacation—from Tennessee to the Grand Canyon, Yellowstone and back, taking the time to see all that they could along the way. They had stopped in Van Buren and gotten a motel room for the night, and after a quick dinner, they returned to the room for some TV and a good night's sleep. They got the TV, but the good night's sleep eluded them.

It had been a long day, and it didn't take long before the kids were fast asleep and Carol's husband was starting to nod off. Turning off the TV and making sure that the bathroom light was on and the door was almost closed, leaving just enough light for the kids to make it to the bathroom in the dark, she turned in as well. She said that something caused her to wake up, maybe a noise or something—she wasn't exactly sure what—but at the time, she thought one of the kids had gotten up. As she sort of half sat up in bed and got her eyes to focus in the darkened room, she could make out the figure of a man standing at the end of the kids' bed, staring at them. She screamed and jumped out of bed, fumbling for the light switch. Her husband, startled by his wife's scream and thinking that something was drastically wrong, jumped up out of bed ready to fight. They both looked directly at the man standing at the foot of the kid's bed and couldn't believe what they saw. Standing there was a man in a Confederate gray uniform. As Carol's husband launched himself across the bed to engage what he thought was an intruder, he passed right through the man and landed in a pile on the floor next to the door. As he got to his feet and spun around, both he and Carol watched the man in the gray uniform simply disappear right in front of their eyes.

They both described the man as being fairly tall, with long stringy hair that poked out from under a dilapidated hat, a full unkempt beard and a pistol tucked into the front of a wide belt. They both thought he looked to be extremely dangerous, with or without the gun. They said he never spoke; he just stood there looking at the kids while they slept and only turned his head to look at either of them when Carol screamed and her husband leaped at him.

I told them that it was a very interesting story and that it sounded like a very exciting experience. They didn't think it was such a cool experience at all and were worried that maybe he might follow them or something. I told them that it sounded like maybe the spirit was just curious about them or maybe he had kids of his own at one time or another and seeing them sleeping held his attention and brought back a memory or something. I asked them if they experienced anything else that night, and they said no, that they had slept with the bathroom door open and the bathroom light on, as well as one of the lamps by the bed. I had to suppress a smile when she told me that she and her husband slept in shifts the rest of the night. Carol said the kids never woke up during any of it—they just kept sleeping, peaceful as could be, while the whole thing was going down.

She asked if I thought they had anything to be worried about, and I told them that I didn't see any indication of anything that should raise any concern. I explained to them that the area around the town had seen some action during the Civil War, and perhaps he had been a casualty of that conflict. There was really no way to tell, but I pointed out that he hadn't tried to harm anyone in any way. She could also think of it as he was just watching over them as they slept to make sure no harm came to them. I told them that the fact that he looked like a dangerous person was simply perception. He didn't look like a modern-day person, and he had a large pistol thrust into his belt; in his day, he would have fit right in with everyone else, but in today's society, he would have looked a little dangerous. All in all, I told them to enjoy their vacation and not to worry about it. I also told them to consider themselves lucky to have experienced it, as a lot of paranormal investigators and researchers have never even seen a full-bodied apparition before. Neither Carol nor her husband saw it that way.

The story told to me by Carol and her husband is the only one I have run across related to the Super 8 Motel. The reason for that, I would think, is that the people who experienced anything would move on with their trips the next morning, taking the stories of their experiences with them. It was just sheer luck that I happened to have my TOPS shirt on and went into the Waffle House to eat at the same time Carol and her family was there. Thirty minutes to an hour either way and our paths might not have crossed, and the story would never have made itself known to me. I wasn't able to find anyone at the motel who would admit to experiencing anything paranormal in nature or who knew of anyone who had an experience similar to Carol's. That doesn't mean that it didn't happen to Carol or that no one else has experienced anything; it just means that the stories have yet to be found. Is the Super 8 Motel haunted? There is no way to determine that without multiple investigations, but it certainly wouldn't be the first haunted hotel in existence.

The Drennen–Scott Home

Located at 221 North Third Street in Van Buren, this home was finished somewhere around 1838 by the founder of Van Buren, John Drennen. It had remained in the ownership of his descendants until it was purchased by the University of Arkansas–Fort Smith in 2005, and after a six-year restoration at a cost of about $5.2 million, the site was opened to the public as a museum and learning center for university students.

The home originally started out as a one-room structure somewhere around 1834 or 1836 and was added on to as the Drennen family grew in size. Drennen's daughter Caroline married a man by the name of Charles Scott, and the property was passed on to them when John Drennen passed away. The site was added to the National Register of Historic Places in 1971.

Today, the home has been restored, is managed by the Historical Interpretation Program of the University of Arkansas and holds many of the original pieces of furniture, business papers and correspondence, as well as a set of twelve solid silver tumblers that John Drennen had made from his horse racing winnings—a pretty impressive collection of artifacts. Unlike a lot of historical sites furnished in period pieces, the Drennen home contains a lot of the original items of the home since the property had always remained in the family.

As one might expect, a home that old and furnished with a lot of original items has a lot of ghost stories to go with it. Some have been known for years, and some have only cropped up since the restorations on the home and

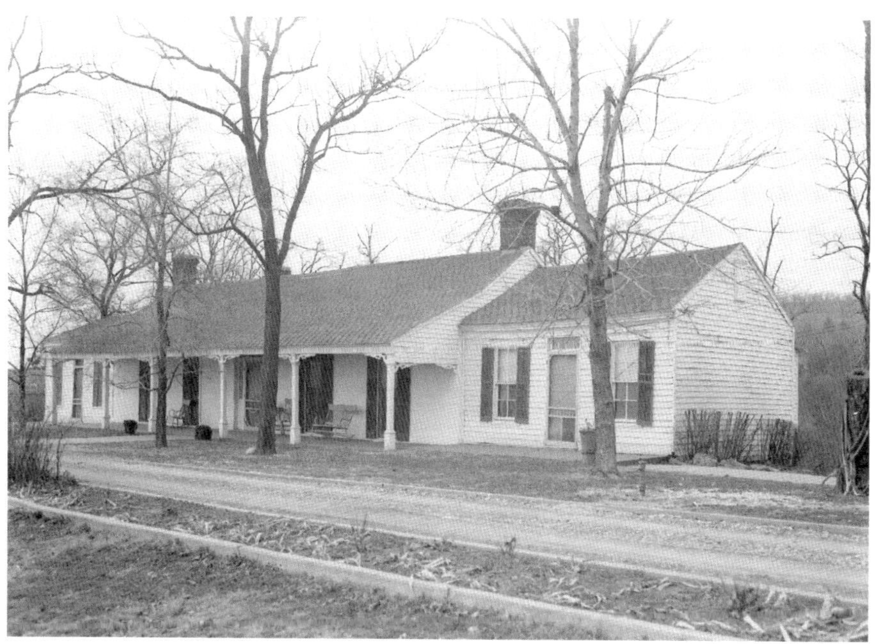

Drennen-Scott House, 1940. *Courtesy of the Library of Congress.*

property began. One can't help but wonder if the alleged spirits associated with the home are attached directly to the property or to some item in the home that they held a particular fondness for—perhaps the spirit of John Drennen himself might still be hanging around because of the silver tumblers. Either way, there seems to be some reason that the home is still occupied by some of its former residents. It could just simply be that it was their home, a place they loved, built and raised their families in—a place of happiness for them.

The Pipe Smoker

One story that I have repeatedly heard over the years is that of the "Pipe Smoker." Sometimes he is seen standing or walking on the porch and other times only footsteps are heard, but the smell of pipe tobacco seems to follow along with the footsteps. Those who have caught a glimpse of the man describe him as being of medium height, about five feet, six or seven inches tall, dressed in what appears to be work clothes and sporting a full, very well-groomed beard. At times he is seen wearing glasses, the little round wire-framed ones, and other times no glasses are present. He seems to be lost in thought when seen, standing on the porch staring off into space or walking back and forth, head down as if in contemplation of some problem.

Just who he might be is anyone's guess. Some have thought that it might be John Drennen himself, keeping watch over the family home, and while it might be true, it could be someone else entirely. He has also been seen around the property as well, out in the yard and on the paths, just walking around and taking it all in. One would have to wonder if it is John Drennen and he is self-aware, which the reports of his interaction with people would lead you to believe, it must be rather confusing for him at times. Everything has been restored to look as it would in his day, yet there would be so many differences that only he might be aware of, not to mention the blatant ones such as interpretive walking paths. It must all make him scratch his head in wonderment at how it is, yet isn't, the same as he would remember it. No wonder he is seen with his head down, apparently lost in thought.

One of the students who work at the site (and is pursuing his bachelor's degree in history) told me about an experience that he had while leading a small group of people on a tour of the walking paths. They had just started out when he noticed an older man with a beard and spectacles had joined the group. He was dressed in old clothes that looked like work clothes. He wondered where the guy had come from but just brushed it off and continued with what he was talking about, moving the small group of people along the path. When they stopped again, he noticed that the man wasn't with the group, which was a bit odd since there really wasn't anywhere that he could go without someone still being able to see him. As he was explaining what that particular interpretive stop was about, he started to smell pipe tobacco. He turned around to tell whoever had lit up a pipe that they weren't allowed to smoke, but no one was there. The other people in the group smelled the pipe tobacco as well, but no one could pinpoint where it was coming from. Deciding that it must be drifting in on the wind, he continued on with the group, moving on to the next stop.

As they approached it, he turned around and was walking backward as he was talking, explaining what the stop was all about. One of the group members told him to watch out and pointed behind him. He stopped and looked around, and there was the man who he had seen in the group, the one who had seemed to disappear at the previous stop. The man was standing there looking at him with what appeared to be a white clay pipe jutting from the corner of his mouth. The young man said, "Excuse me," more out of reflex than anything, and then asked the man how he had gotten there. He also told the man that smoking was prohibited on the property and that he would have to extinguish his pipe or he would be asked to leave. The older man just smiled at him, took the pipe out of his mouth and said, "Son, I'm not going anywhere at all." And with that, the man turned around, took a few steps down the path and faded from sight. He said everyone in the group was speechless for a moment, and then an excited chatter started up. He was absolutely baffled by what had just happened. He said that he tried to continue on with the group, but no one was listening. They were to busy talking about the ghost with the pipe.

He told me that he never saw the man again, but from time to time, he would smell pipe tobacco around him as if someone were following him around smoking a pipe. He said it was more annoying than spooky since he never cared for the smell of tobacco at all.

Grandpa John

One lady I spoke with, of all places at the Van Buren Waffle House again (I'm starting to see a pattern develop here), told me that she grew up close to the old Drennen-Scott Home. As kids, they used to play on the property. One afternoon about midsummer, she and her brother and a younger sister were playing in the trees that surrounded the property. She said that Miss Caroline didn't care that they played there as long as they didn't tear anything up. Well, they were running around in the timberline playing hide-and-seek when she almost ran full tilt into an older gentleman. She said one minute there was empty space and the next minute he was standing there. She apologized and said, "Excuse me, sir," to which the man looked at her and smiled. He told her it was okay, that it wasn't the first time someone had almost ran into him. As the other kids gathered around, he then asked her what they were doing there. She explained that they were playing games and that Miss Caroline had said it was okay for them to play there. The man chuckled and said, "Well, if Caroline said it was okay, then it must be okay." He then told them to be careful and to watch out for Caroline's flowerbeds, that she "wouldn't take kindly to getting her flowers all tore up." With that, he smiled at the kids, nodded his head and turned to leave. The kids all looked at one another and turned back around to ask him what his name was, but he was nowhere to be seen. They ran around the trees looking for him, but he had disappeared from sight. She said the kids just went back to playing, but as she got older, she started to wonder just where the man had gone. There was nowhere that he could have hidden since the trees had been thinned out and the underbrush was cut pretty low.

She said that she was so bothered by how the man disappeared and by who he might be that she paid a visit to Miss Caroline to ask her if she might know who he was. As she described the man and told the story to Miss Caroline, she said that she started to smile and chuckled just a bit. Caroline looked at her and said, "Child, you just saw an old ghost was all. It sounds like you saw Grandpa John. We've seen him around the place for as long as I can remember." With that, she told her not to worry. He wouldn't harm anyone; he just likes staying at home.

She said she visited with Miss Caroline for a bit longer and then went on back home. They continued to play games in the trees until they got too old to play such things, their interests turning to school friends and the start of a budding social life. She said she never forgot the man. He seemed to be a kind person. He smiled and talked to the kids in a nice way and didn't holler at them for being there. I asked her if she had visited the place since it had been restored, and she said that she had visited it once, that they had done such a nice job in fixing it up, but that she probably wouldn't go back again. It was just too hard for her to do all that walking. When I spoke to her, she told me that she had been born in Van Buren in 1946 and had lived there for most of her life. She was seventy-one years old when I talked with her, and she proudly exclaimed, "Oh, the changes I've seen in this place!" She was an absolute delight to visit with.

There are a lot of interesting stories associated with the Drennen-Scott House, some a bit more believable than others but interesting just the same. Over the years, people have reported hearing footsteps inside the house and on the porch, items being moved around on tables, the disembodied sounds of conversation and the occasional glimpse of a shadowy type of figure in the trees. There have also been a large number of instances where people smelled tobacco smoke, even when there was no one smoking and no smoke even visible. Phantom smells are not that unusual, and investigators and researchers have been encountering the smells of tobacco, perfume and, in some cases, food for as long as I can remember. It also seems as if a lot of the reported footsteps and disembodied voices picked up in volume after the renovations started—something else that isn't that unusual. There have been numerous cases investigated where a homeowner or building owner had started renovations only to start experiencing an upturn in paranormal activity. In a very few cases, the activity took a violent turn, with hammers, wood and other things being tossed about the place—in some cases tossed at the workers. Perhaps the activity of doing a remodel stirs them up because of change. Their environment is changing, which takes them out of their comfort zone, so to speak. No one really knows for sure why the increase happens, but I have always found the correlation between remodeling/renovations and increased paranormal activity to be worthy of further investigation.

CRAWFORD COUNTY COURTHOUSE

With the original section of the courthouse being built in 1842, the Crawford County Courthouse is believed to be the oldest operating courthouse west of the Mississippi River. It is situated on a section of ground donated by John Drennen and David Thompson on the condition that the county courthouse is always located in Van Buren.

The courthouse has seen a lot of history since it was built, as well as some hard usage. During the Civil War and the Battle of Van Buren, the building was saved from destruction, although all of the records from 1855 to 1860 that were kept there were burned. A running battle between the retreating Confederates and the pursuing Union troops was waged right down the main street of the town and past the courthouse. Confederate artillery shelled the town before being driven back by the Union artillery placed on the high ground at Fairview Cemetery; the old courthouse emerged unscathed from the artillery attack. It wasn't so lucky in 1877 though. Arsonists set fire to the building and pretty much gutted it. The courthouse was rebuilt using the existing walls that had escaped the damage of the fire; again, however, most of the records were destroyed.

The grounds of the courthouse hold several things of interest to anyone interested in history. Around 1906, the statue commemorating the Confederate dead was moved from Fairview Cemetery to the courthouse grounds. A few years later, the Women's Village Improvement Society, through funds raised by the Women's League of Van Buren, placed a gold-painted iron statue of the Greek goddess Hebe, the goddess of youth and

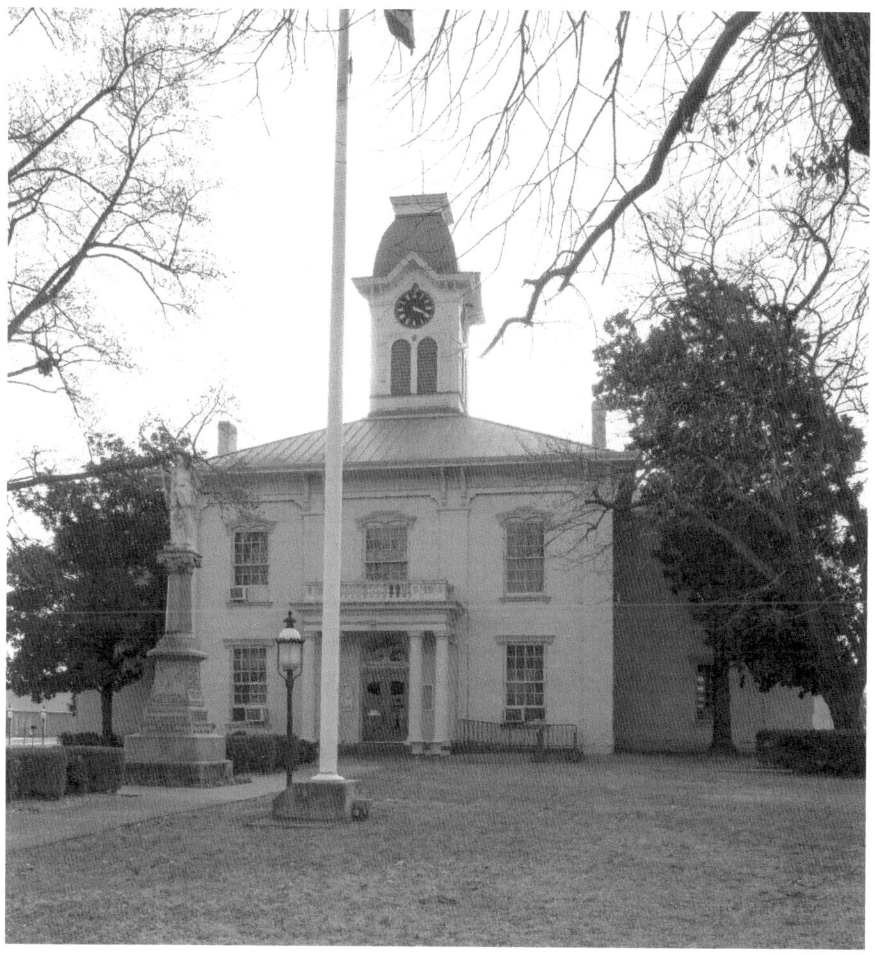

Front view of the historic Crawford County Courthouse. *Photo by Bud Steed.*

happiness, on the courthouse lawn in 1908. The original statue was starting to show signs of wear, and it was replaced with a new bronze cast statue in 2003. The original was placed in the Crawford County Museum. You can find the 1832 log cabin schoolhouse used by Albert Pike on the courthouse grounds too. Pike was a teacher, poet, writer, politician, and Freemason. He was also a Confederate general who served in the Battle of Pea Ridge in northwest Arkansas.

The old courthouse served as a stop on the Butterfield stage line, which ran between St. Louis, Missouri, and San Francisco, California. The stage route

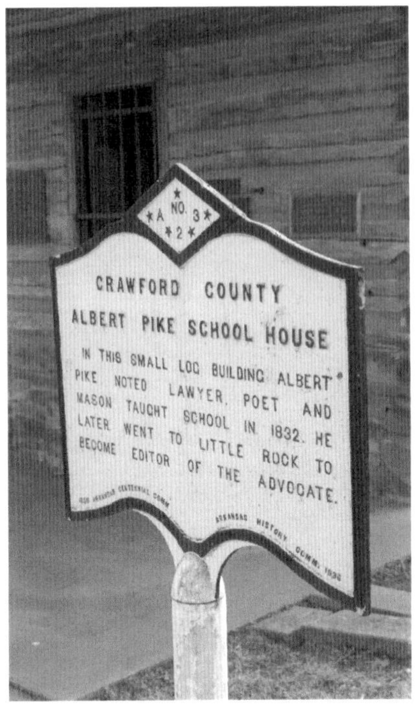

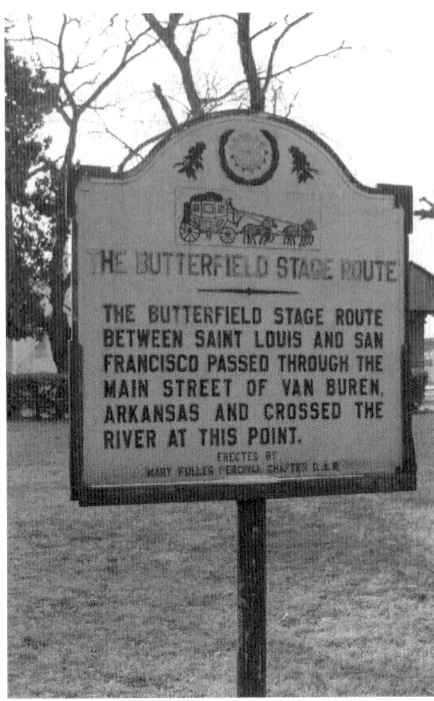

Left: Sign commemorating Albert Pike, located in front of the log schoolhouse. *Photo by Bud Steed.*

Right: Sign commemorating the Butterfield Stage route. It passed right in front of the courthouse and crossed the river at the end of Main Street. *Photo by Bud Steed.*

passed right down Van Buren's Main Street, and a marker commemorating it is located on the courthouse lawn. The building and the ground around it have seen a lot of history pass by. It's little wonder that some people claim that a bit of that history stuck around.

Albert Pike's Schoolhouse

The little log schoolhouse sits just a few yards from the courthouse and is pretty much open to the elements. When I visited it, the door was wide open, although a steel gate covered the doorway to keep people from walking in. It was evident that it had seen some disrepair over the years. Now, don't get me wrong, it wasn't falling apart or falling in or anything,

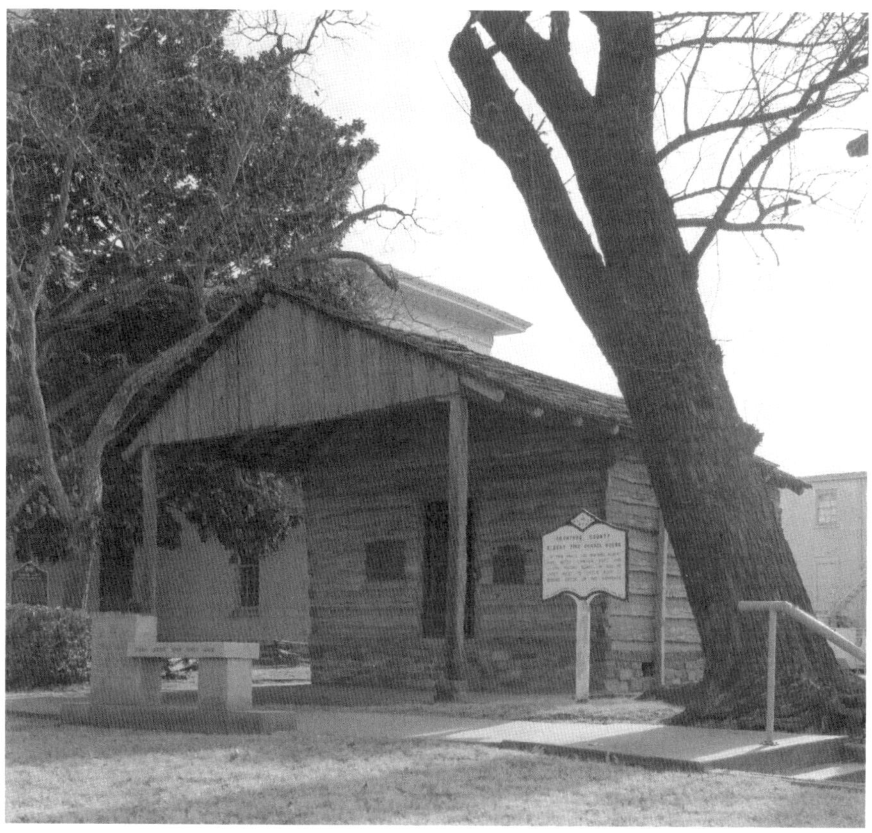

Log cabin schoolhouse where Albert Pike taught for a brief period of time before moving to Little Rock. Pike was a general in the Confederate army and was also a noted Freemason. *Photo by Bud Steed.*

but you could tell that it was showing its age a little bit and could have used some restoration.

I was struck by just how small the one-room schoolhouse was and tried to imagine a bunch of kids all wedged in there trying to learn. But my perception was flawed, as not every kid went to school back then, and the place wasn't really overrun with kids either. In retrospect, it was probably just the right size to fit the need.

I've heard several accounts associated with the log schoolhouse, one of which I'm not sure belongs with the log structure so much as it does the ground around it. A few people have reported seeing a Confederate soldier, complete with rucksack and rifle, run inside the schoolhouse through the wall by the front door and then disappear. When I first heard the story,

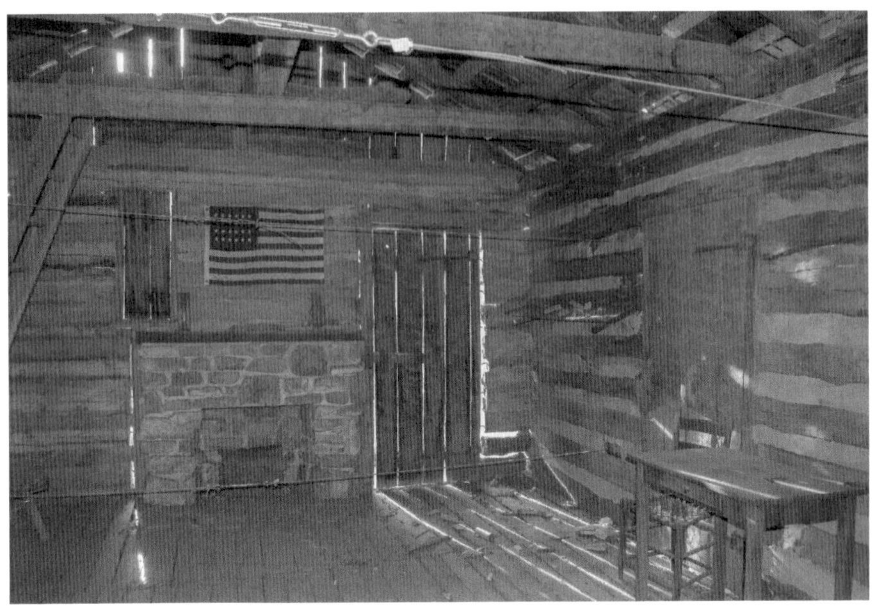

Interior view of the log schoolhouse. It was moved to the courthouse grounds from its original location and reconstructed. *Photo by Bud Steed.*

I wondered why he would run into the schoolhouse in the first place and through the wall. Then it occurred to me that he wasn't really running into it; he was just running, probably during the Battle of Van Buren, and he most likely wasn't anything more than a residual type of entity that had no idea the schoolhouse was even there. He was still replaying his escape from the Union troops, time and again; it's the only explanation that makes any sense to me. I've heard of hauntings where spirits would walk up a flight of stairs that wasn't there or through a wall, and after some research, it was discovered that there had been a stairway and a door there at one point. The spirit was just going through the motions as if it was still there. To me, that's the running soldier seen going through the schoolhouse wall.

Another story that was told to me is of a man seen walking out of the schoolhouse door (which means he walked through the steel gate), pausing for a moment to place a hat on his head and fading from sight. The whole thing happens in just a few seconds and leaves the witness wondering if they actually saw it or not.

Several people have also seen a flickering light moving around inside the log structure in the very early morning hours as if someone was walking around carrying a candle. When investigated, the light goes out, and no one is found either inside or outside the building. The smell of wood smoke has also been noted around the log schoolhouse, although I would point out that the structure does have a wood-burning fireplace that has obviously seen a lot of use over the years, and the smell could simply be the smell of charred wood or wood smoke built up over the years and left inside the chimney walls. All in all, it's a pretty interesting log schoolhouse, and it's impressive that it has survived all of these years, but I'm not so sure about the alleged ghost sightings.

The Man in the Hallway

A young lady by the name of Janelle shared this story with me while I was walking around the inside of the old courthouse checking it out. (It's pretty cool inside too, by the way.) She works in one of the offices in the building and asked me if there was anything she could help me with—apparently I looked a little lost and out of place. After I told her who I was and why I was there, she shared this story with me.

A year or so earlier, she had just finished her first week working in the building, and she was glad to get through it. It was difficult, to say the least; she didn't know her way around, was unfamiliar with how her job was supposed to go and just felt a little overwhelmed the entire week. She said that her coworkers had all been supportive of her and told her not to worry about it, that she would catch on. But she still felt like she was failing anyway.

She had stayed late to try and finish up what she was behind on, so everyone else in her office had left already; for that matter, most of the people in the building had left too. She closed the office door behind her, making sure it was locked, and then walked down the hallway a short distance to one of the benches and plopped down. She said that she felt totally exhausted, and she leaned back against the bench and closed her eyes for a moment. She said she took a few deep breaths, opened her eyes and was startled to find an older-looking gentleman sitting on the bench next to her. She said she just about jumped three feet in the air.

The man apologized for startling her and asked her if she was okay. She said she didn't know why she did it—maybe because he reminded her of her grandfather or something—but the next thing she knew she was spilling her guts to him about how worried she was about her job, how her week went, that she was afraid her reputation as a good worker would be tarnished if she failed and everything else, tears included. The old man just sat there smiling at her and nodding his head from time to time, listening intently to everything she had to say. When she was finished, she realized what she had done and apologized for dumping her problems and worries all over him. She said she felt so embarrassed.

The old man smiled at her, patted her hand and told her it would all be okay. Janelle said he turned a little on the seat, looked straight at her and said, "Kid, the fact that you stayed and stuck it out speaks volumes about your character. Your reputation isn't who you are; it's what people think you are. It's your character that defines you. You just keep after it, keep working hard and do the right thing, and it will all be okay."

With that, the old man patted her hand again and got up off the bench. As he started to walk away, he turned back around, waved at her and said, "See you around, kid." Janelle smiled and waved back and then looked down at her purse to get another tissue. When she looked back up, he was gone. That's when she realized that she hadn't heard him approach, sit down or even walk away. He hadn't made any noise in the empty hallway. There also wasn't anywhere for him to disappear to, as all of the offices were closed and locked and they were quite a ways away from the stairs. She said she just sat there for a moment wondering if she had imagined it all, but deep inside, she knew that she hadn't. She's certain to this day that the old man she spoke with and who gave her such sound advice was a ghost; no one will ever convince her otherwise. She told me that she has worked at the courthouse for quite some time now and has never seen the man again—not there, not around town, not anywhere else. She also told me that if she hadn't spoken with him that evening and gotten those words of encouragement from him, she probably wouldn't have come back to work the next Monday.

The Crawford County Courthouse is one of those places that you would expect to have a lot of paranormal activity associated with, a place that would have some good stories considering the history it has witnessed. But other than Janelle's story and the reports associated with the little log schoolhouse, I wasn't able to dig up a whole lot past the usual stuff.

A lot of people have remarked over the years about hearing loud footsteps in the hallway, some of them leading right up to their office door, but there never seems to be anyone there when they go look. The sounds of muted conversation are also heard, but being an old building with hallways that tend to echo a little bit, I can't help but wonder how much of that muted conversation might be coming from another floor or from somewhere else within the building.

I did find one account of a person claiming to have seen a man with a satchel suddenly appear on the stairs. He stood there for a moment like he was lost and then bolted up a few feet of stairs before disappearing. Curiously, he didn't make any sounds as he was moving either, although he was described as a young man in a very nice suit and didn't resemble the description of the old man Janelle encountered.

For what it's worth, while I was walking around checking out the inside of the courthouse, I didn't feel any type of energy associated with anything bad—the kind you run into that makes the hair stand up on your arms and the back of your neck. Inside, everything felt just as it should—a peaceful courthouse where everyone was busy at their jobs. Outside, though, it was an entirely different story. You could walk around outside, both up close to the building and farther out into the yard, and come upon spots where it was noticeably cooler and the hair on your neck and arms would stand up. Maybe they were nothing more than depressions of air that were a bit cooler than the air around it, but that wouldn't explain the energy charge that you could feel. Perhaps each one marked the spot where a Civil War soldier fell during the Battle of Van Buren, but we have no way of knowing that for sure. But one thing is for certain: the exterior of the building has an entirely different feel than the interior.

CONCLUSION

Fort Smith, Van Buren and the areas around them have a lot of interesting stories to tell. The ones that I've included in this book are just a few of them, and I included some stories that are pretty well known, as well as some that aren't, in the hopes of inspiring readers to get out and do a little research about their area themselves. Whether it's the area covered in this book or somewhere else entirely, every place has some type of unique story associated with it, some ghost story or lost legend just begging for someone to dig into it and discover the reason why it started; the history of a place will provide that for you in most cases, and that's why I love what I do.

I've enjoyed writing this book immensely. The subject matter is one that really captures my attention—the history, the local legends and the ghost stories. The area has plenty of both, and they certainly will not disappoint you in the slightest. While some of the stories might be questionable at best, they are entertaining and show how some people believe in a connection with the supernatural. Some people get freaked out, like Carol and her husband, while others, like the feisty old guy I met by Fairview Cemetery, seem to take it all in stride and accept it for what it is.

There is one thing that I would like to say that I hope people will take to heart. I don't want to come across as preachy, but this is about one thing: preservation. We, all of us, need to be more conscious of preserving our historical buildings and sites. We need to take an active roll in documenting and preserving them for our future generations because no matter how hard we might try, nothing lasts forever. There are lots of ways that you can help too. You can volunteer at a historical site, help out and support a historical society or even get out and take some photographs of historic sites in your area and then offer them to your local historical society or to the Library of Congress. There are lots of ways to get involved, and I hope that you will take the time to do so.

I would also like to leave you with this final piece of advice. If this book has inspired you to get out and do a paranormal investigation of your own or even to get out and document some old places, never go alone. As my grandfather used to say to me when I was a kid, "Boy, it's not the dead you have to worry about; it's the living that will hurt you." Sound advice then and sound advice now. There are some basic safety rules that everyone needs to follow to make sure that you come home safe and sound to those who love and care for you. This list is by no means complete, and you should add to it to suit your own individual situation.

- Never go alone. Always take someone with you because you never know what might happen. You could fall and get hurt, get trapped in an old building or any number of things. Do not go it alone!
- Make sure your cell phone is fully charged. In an emergency, it could be the difference between getting help or dying alone, trapped in some old decrepit basement of an abandoned house. Not a cool situation at all.
- Make sure you tell someone who is *not* going with you where you are going to be and approximately how long you will be gone and set a check-in time for you to call them. Instruct them that if they don't hear from you by fifteen minutes after the agreed-on check-in time, they are to try calling you. If they get no answer, instruct them to call the police. Better safe than sorry.
- Always carry extra flashlight batteries and something to eat and drink. I carry a few granola bars and a bottle of water in my gear bag every time I go out.
- Hide a spare key somewhere on the outside of your car, like in one of those magnetic key holders. The last thing you want is to be out in the middle of nowhere or in a sketchy neighborhood and realize that you've lost your keys.

Like I said, this is not a complete list and you can adapt it to your situation, but it is a good starting point. You can find this same list, as well as other information, on my websites. You can go to budsteed.com or backroadsparanormal.com to check it all out. If you enjoyed this book, I would invite you to check out my other books at arcadiapublishing.com/Home or on Amazon.

Until next time, stay safe and happy haunting!

BIBLIOGRAPHY

Images

Scalf, A.S. Various Fort Smith Arkansas images, Fort Smith, Arkansas, March 4, 2018.

Online and Print Sources

Boulden, B. "The Lynching of Sanford Lewis." Fort Smith History. https://www.fortsmithhistory.org/archive/lynchingSL.html.

Chester House Inn and Antiques. "Chester AR Real Haunt." https://www.arkansashauntedhouses.com/real-haunt/chester-house-inn-antiques.html.

Christ, M.K. "Fairview Cemetery—Confederate Section." Encyclopedia of Arkansas. http://www.encyclopediaofarkansas.net/encyclopedia/entry-detail.aspx?entryID=8639.

City of Van Buren, Arkansas. "Fairview Cemetery Design Guidelines." https://www.vanburencity.org/DocumentCenter/Home/View/101.

Clayton House. "Belle Grove Historic District." http://claytonhouse.org/history/belle-grove-historic-district.

———. "The Historic Home." http://claytonhouse.org/history/the-historic-home.

———. "William Henry Harrison Clayton." http://claytonhouse.org/history/william-henry-harrison-clayton.

Cox, D. "The Battle of Van Buren." Explore Southern History. http://www.exploresouthernhistory.com/vanburenbattle1.html.

———. "Crawford County Courthouse—A Civil War Landmark in Van Buren, Arkansas." Civil War Arkansas. http://civilwararkansas.blogspot.com/2012/04/crawford-county-courthouse-civil-war.html.

———. "Fairview Cemetery." Civil War Arkansas. http://civilwararkansas.blogspot.com/2009/03/fairview-cemetery-van-buren-arkansas.html.

Demaret, K. "Plagued by Heat, Crime and Snafus, the Fort Chaffee Refugee Camp Becomes an American Nightmare." *People*. http://people.com/archive/plagued-by-heat-crime-and-snafus-the-fort-chaffee-refugee-camp-becomes-an-american-nightmare-vol-14-no-1.

The Department of Arkansas Heritage. "Clayton House." http://www.arkansasheritage.com/blog/clayton-house.

Explore Southern History. "Battle of Massard Prairie." http://www.exploresouthernhistory.com/ArkansasCW4.html.

———. "Fairview Cemetery—Van Buren, Arkansas." 2011. http://www.exploresouthernhistory.com/fairviewcemetery.html.

Fort Smith, Arkansas. "Massard Prairie Battlefield Park." https://www.fortsmith.org/massard-prairie-battlefield-park.

Fort Smith History. "Marquardt's Ghost Returns Christmas." https://www.fortsmithhistory.org/archive/marquardt.html. Originally published in the *Fort Smith News Record* on December 27, 1903.

Fort Smith Museum. http://www.fortsmithmuseum.org.

Freeman, W. Van Buren (Crawford County). Encyclopedia of Arkansas. http://www.encyclopediaofarkansas.net/encyclopedia/entry-detail.aspx?entryID=868.

Gorham, J. "Haunted Arkansas: The Phantom of the King Opera House." *Fort Smith/Fayetteville News*, October 30, 2012. http://5newsonline.com/2012/10/30/haunted-arkansas-the-phantom-of-the-king-opera-house.

Music of the 1890s from the Erdmann Collection. http://www.parlorsongs.com/issues/2010-11/thismonth/feature.php.

National Cemetery Administration. https://www.cem.va.gov/cems/nchp/ftsmith.asp.

National Park Service. "History and Culture." August 28, 2017. https://www.nps.gov/fosm/learn/historyculture/index.htm.

Spears, L. "Drennen-Scott Historic Site." Encyclopedia of Arkansas, March 22, 2017. http://www.encyclopediaofarkansas.net/encyclopedia/entry-detail.aspx?entryID=6945.

University of Arkansas–Fort Smith. "Drennen-Scott House." http://class.uafs.edu/history/drennen-scott-house.

Van Buren. "History of Van Buren." http://www.van-buren.com/history.html.

Van Buren, Arkansas. "The King Opera House." http://www.vanburen.org/attractions/king-opera-house.

Walton-Raji, A.Y. "United States Colored Troops of Crawford County, Ark." Arkansas Freedmen of the Frontier, January 10, 2010. http://www.arkansasfreedmen.com/usctcrawford.html.

About the Author

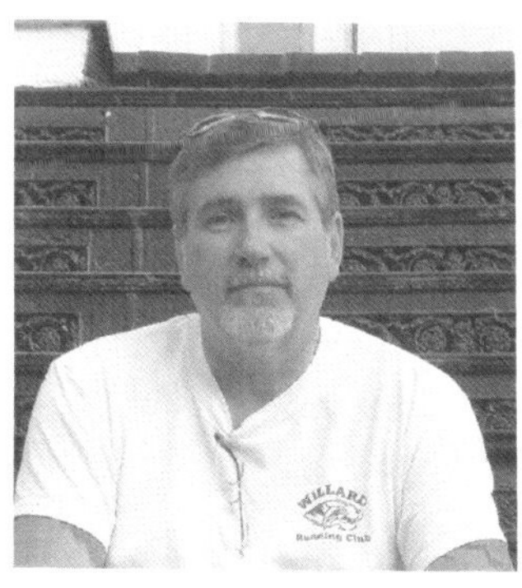

Bud Steed is an author, researcher, paranormal investigator and explorer of strange and lost legends; if it's strange, weird or kind of scary, he's probably interested in it. So far, he has written and published six books: *Haunted Natchez Trace*, *Haunted Mississippi Gulf Coast*, *Haunted Baton Rouge*, *Haunted Northwest Arkansas*, *Ozarks Ghosts and Hauntings* and a book on treasure legends called *Lost Treasures of the Ozarks*. His books contain a lot of history, and it is his belief that each ghost story, legend or strange occurrence has its roots buried somewhere in historical fact. Researching the history behind the story gives the reader a better sense of why the legend or ghost sighting started in the first place and allows both the reader and the investigator to separate the fact from the fiction, hopefully leading them down the twisting, turning path to the truth.

Bud has been researching the paranormal for more than thirty-eight years and has investigated in both Europe and the United States. He is the founder of Backroads Paranormal, a team dedicated to investigating historical sites and small-town legends, and is the co-founder of Infinity Paranormal Research.

In 2011, along with fellow researcher Dave Harkins and additional team members from The Ozarks Paranormal Society, he investigated the Historic

Ray House and Wilson's Creek National Battlefield. Theirs was the first team to receive a federally sanctioned permit to conduct an overnight paranormal investigation. The investigation was filmed for the Travel Channel show *Legends of the Ozarks* and produced interesting evidence of the hauntings associated with the battlefield. He has also participated in several other film projects, one concerning the Natchez Trace for the series *Deadly Possessions* and the other concerning strange stories and legends associated with the Mark Twain National Forest for the series *Mysteries of the Outdoors*.

He is currently working on several more book projects, as well as filming multiple paranormal investigations of historical sites for a project on haunted history.

Currently, he resides in the beautiful Ozark Mountains of southwest Missouri with his amazingly patient wife, Jennifer; four great kids, David, Sean, Ciara Jo and Kerra Lynn; and two pit bulls named Dixie and Clyde.

Bud is available for events, book signings, and speaking engagements and can be contacted at bud@budsteed.com.

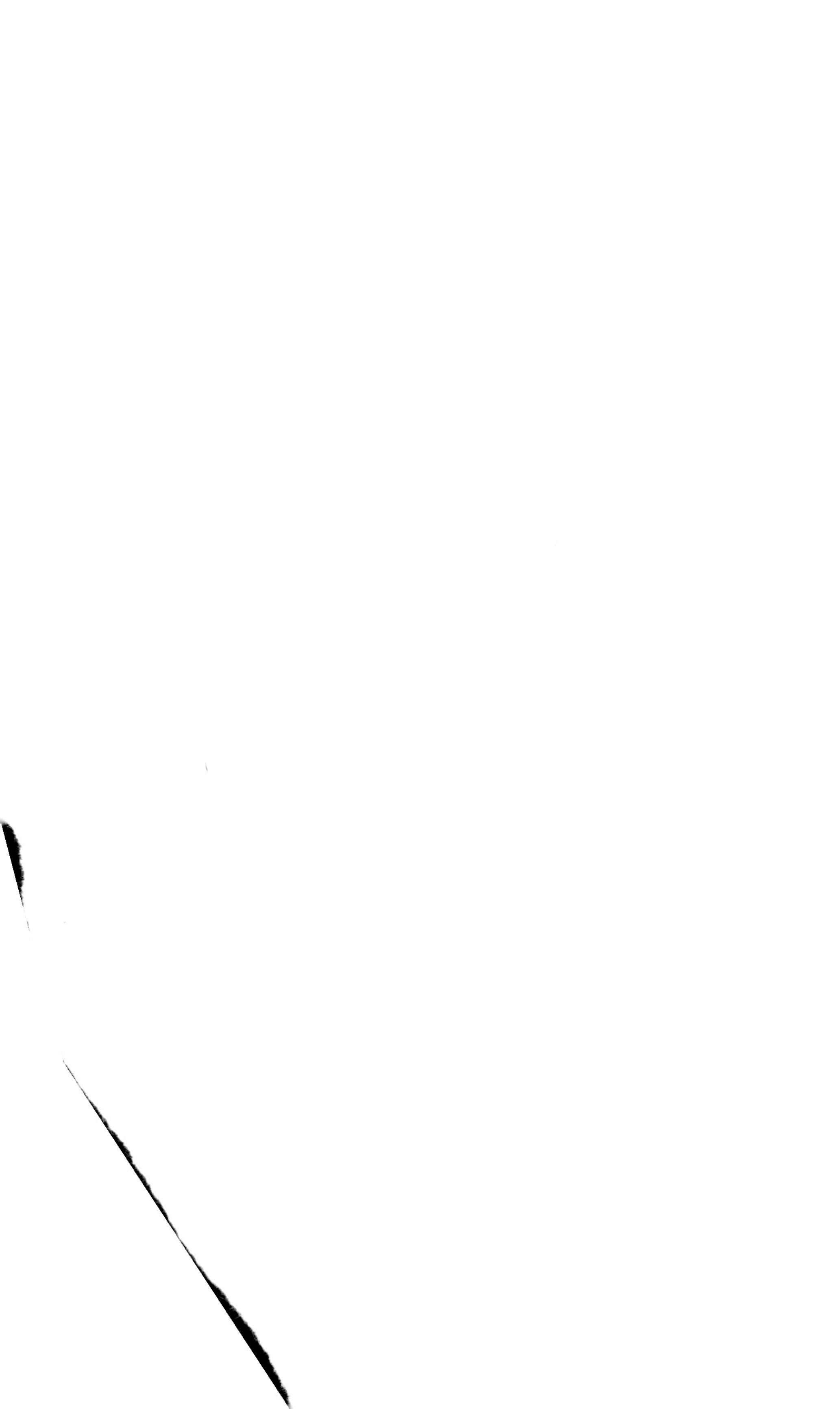

Visit us at
www.historypress.com